# TEAM UP

Cover design by Lauren Shay, Full Stop Publishing
Illustrations by Alison Zammit
Layout by Lorna Hendry
Edited by Lu Sexton


Luiters, Keegan
Team Up
ISBN 9780648917106 (Print)
ISBN 9780648917113 (ebook)

Disclaimer
The material in this publication is of the nature of general comment only and does not represent professional advice. It is not intended to provide specific guidance for any particular circumstances and it should not be relied upon for any decision to take action or not to take action on any matter which it covers. Readers should obtain professional advice where appropriate, before making any such decision. To the maximum extent permitted by law, the author and publisher disclaim all responsibility and liability to any person, arising directly or indirectly from any person taking or not taking action based on the information in this book.

# TEAM UP

Take a deliberate approach
to team performance.

**KEEGAN LUITERS**

For Alia

Have fun. Be kind. Be curious.

# ABOUT THE AUTHOR

Keegan Luiters is an experienced presenter, facilitator and coach with a Masters Degree in Business Coaching. He has spent his life in and around teams, leadership, learning and performance.

His background includes semi-professional cricket with and against some of the best cricketers in the world in Australia and the UK, as well as marathon running. He brings this passion for teams, leadership, learning and performance to the work that he does.

He has almost two decades of experience working with organisations in Australia and New Zealand across organisations ranging from small business, government agencies and not-for-profit organisations through to large corporate organisations. His experience includes working with KPMG, Westpac, THE ICONIC, Green Building Council of Australia, Henry William Lawyers, Delta Group, Wideform, Verdia and AFL among others.

He lives in Sydney with his wife and daughter. When not delivering programs, coaching or writing, you will probably find him engaging with one of his mild addictions – family, food, friends, caffeine, dad jokes or trying to improve his golf (which is probably a mild addiction as well).

# ACKNOWLEDGEMENTS

Writing a book is a process full of highs, lows, frustrations and excitement. The process is something that I am very grateful to have gone through and not one that I have done alone. This book talks about how almost nothing that we achieve is done alone and this book is an example of that.

Firstly, I'd like to acknowledge the most important team in my life. Thanks so much to my wife, Rebecca. Your support, guidance and feedback have always been what I needed. You have shown remarkable patience with me as I dedicated time to this process. Thanks to my awesome daughter, Alia. Due to COVID-19, much of this book has been written on the desk in your room. You constantly show me the value of being human simply by being who you are.

Thanks to the team who took my words and turned them into this book. It's a long way from a word document to the final version. Thanks to Lu Sexton for your editing prowess and sharpening up the messages. You have made sure that the key messages are clear, accessible and easier to navigate. Thanks to my friend, Alison for the illustrations – you add such value to the work and are a pleasure to work with. Thanks to Lorna Hendry for typesetting and Stephanie Preston for proofreading.

Finally, thank you to the leaders, teams and organisations that I work with. It is a privilege to do the work with you. I hope that this book helps that work live on further and longer.

# CONTENTS

# PREFACE

I began writing this book before the COVID-19 pandemic hit, but it seems even more relevant now having lived through these experiences. What a time to be alive! Together, we have experienced some of the most significant and rapid changes in our lives.

The events of 2020 – while intense and in many ways unprecedented – present us with an opportunity that we may not have wished for (or even imagined to be possible), but we can also not deny. Many of the assumptions that we have been operating with have been challenged – and some have been exposed as a reflection of our experiences and preferences rather than as an accurate representation of what is possible.

We have seen this from a number of angles and at different levels – from very personal through to global. What this offers us is the opportunity to consider our own views of what we are experiencing and how we want this experience to shape the way that we operate individually, as business leaders and as a part of the societies that we are interdependent upon.

Our assumptions about the stability of many businesses have been challenged. We have seen large and well established companies forced to dig deep into their reserves and scale back their operations – in some cases towards the edge of administration and beyond. What has become apparent is that we need to be able to operate in more responsive and adaptable ways. We need to be able to design resilience into our ways of working.

The COVID-19 pandemic has heightened the awareness of our interconnected way of living. Because of the amount of travel that we do for business and leisure, this pandemic has been able to spread rapidly to all continents. Commercially and more locally, the impacts have been felt across almost every sector of our economy from hospitality, retail, higher education to real estate and professional services. Our assumptions that we are robust and resilient alone are being stretched.

When, how and where work is getting done has changed, and possibly forever.

I was speaking to a friend and client (same person) who is a partner at one of the big four global consulting firms. As the health and economic implications of the pandemic were becoming evident, he said the following: 'Teamwork is more relevant now than ever'.

He's right. As we explored this, we realised that this was true at many levels. You can see the principles of teamwork are increasingly valuable at different scales:

- Our work teams will benefit from us working collectively, sharing information and staying connected despite being remote.
- Our organisations will benefit from our teams operating more cohesively across departments and divisions.
- Our cities will benefit from us all making sacrifices and taking decisions that put all of us before any one of us (and choosing not to stockpile toilet paper).

- Our nations will benefit from health and economic decisions that rely on different sectors cooperating with each other – suppliers, health workers, schools, transport as well as business.
- Our world will benefit from countries moving away from a nationalistic approach and taking a more holistic approach to the recovery and learning to be better prepared for these events on a global scale.

No single company, industry or even country will recover alone. Our world is interconnected and interdependent.

In many ways, that is the core message of this book. That we are interconnected and interdependent at different scales – and that teamwork matters. The ability to be able to work in a way that applies the principles of teams – interdependent groups with complementary skills and a shared purpose – has always been important. This has been true for thousands of years. Humans occupy the position on the planet that we do because of our ability to be better collectively than independently. If we can tap into the elements of humanity that allow this, our teams and organisations benefit.

# INTRODUCTION

If you are responsible for developing leaders or leading teams yourself, this book is for you.

You will know that these have been challenging responsibilities for a long time, but at the moment it is getting harder. The world is moving fast, expectations of leaders and teams are high and the ability to commit time, money and resources dedicated to developing seems to be shrinking.

It's not just you who is busy. The leaders and teams that you support are also being asked to do more with less. Every person in the organisation is working harder and longer. Individuals are committed and dedicated to achieving their objectives, delivering on their projects and hitting their deadlines. Yet, it's still not enough to keep up with the pace that customers, competitors and technology demand.

You know that your people need to move from being individually busy to collectively productive. You know you need to find new ways of working that are resilient, flexible and adaptable by design – not as an admirable intention.

And you know that resolving these challenges needs a different way of approaching performance and collaboration. But you don't know where to start. Or maybe you've made a number of starts – invested in some team building programs or leadership development initiatives – but you haven't hit upon an approach that will make a significant and lasting shift for you and the people that you work with.

You're not alone.

In my workshops with senior leaders I often start with an exercise that asks them to answer two simple questions about team performance on a scale from *strongly disagree* to *strongly agree*.

1. Is it important?
2. Are you good at it?

I am yet to find a leader who disagrees that team performance is important. Most of the time they are towards the *strongly agree* region. No surprises there. Most of them also tend towards disagreeing with the statement that their teams are good at it. No surprises. Supporting team performance is hard, challenging work.

When I ask the following question, 'Do you have a deliberate approach to team performance?' I also tend to have a consistent response: most of them don't. And this is the core of the problems.

## If you don't have a deliberate approach to team performance, how are you going to support your leaders to operate in high performing teams?

## TEAMS DON'T BECOME TEAMS SIMPLY BECAUSE WE CALL THEM ONE

Simply bringing together a group of talented, hardworking and dedicated individuals is not enough. What is required involves acknowledging that teams are more than a group of skilled people thrown together. Teams require a way of working that allows them to produce something together better than what they could do independently. And that's what this book is going to show you.

I'm going to step you through the Team Performance System, which is a deliberate approach to team performance that takes leadership development and performance development from an event into a way of working.

## NOT JUST ANOTHER TEAM BUILDING PROGRAM

You may have tried some sort of team building program in the past, so let me tell you how my approach differs from many others. Two distinctions underpin the work that I do:

1. I explicitly explore principles relevant *across* teams, not just that team at that time.
2. I acknowledge the fact that leaders are typically on more than one team at any given time.

A system with principles that are applicable *across* teams means that the benefits are broader and longer lasting. The impact applies not just to one particular team at that specific time. The principles allow for improved performance as team composition changes over time, as well as for the multiple teams that leaders are typically a part of at any given time. Which brings me to the second point of difference. Leadership development most often considers team performance in the context of the team that each leader is the appointed hierarchical leader for, it doesn't explore the fact that most leaders are on multiple teams – as project sponsor, subject matter expert, adviser, mentor, manager and more. When leaders are able to add value in all of the teams that they are a part of there are benefits for everyone:

- The work becomes more rewarding for the individual leaders.
- The teams that they contribute to lift their performance.
- Organisations collaborate better cross-functionally.

## HOW TO USE THIS BOOK

My greatest wish for you reading this book is that it gives guidance about useful actions to take – for you, as well as the leaders and teams that you support. For that reason, each chapter has reflective questions that you can ask of yourself and your teams to gain insight into their performance. There are also activities for you to run that will support your teams' development.

There are multiple ways that you can get value out of this book. Read it all at once (to immerse yourself in the concepts), dip in and out of it (for specific information or activities), come back to it often or occasionally (as a reminder or to share with others) – use it in a way that serves you.

To help you navigate, this book is presented in three sections.

- What was (Part I)
- What is (Part II)
- What will be (Part III)

**WHAT WAS**

Part I looks at the forces that have shaped the way that teams operate in our organisations. I will ask you to consider whether these are still relevant for the 2020s. What are the assumptions under which you are trying to get performance out of the teams that you are a part of? Are they relevant for the 2020s and beyond or are they based on models that worked for a world that no longer exists?

**WHAT IS**

Part II is about giving you a way to see teams as they are – not as they were or as we want them to be. We need to see teams as complex, dynamic human systems rather than static or predictable structures. You will be able to dive into the components of the Team Performance System, which I've designed to help you do exactly that.

**WHAT WILL BE**

Finally, Part III explores what will be in our teams. What will be for teams that can combine high levels of each element within the Team Performance System. What will be required of teams as we predict what is coming over the horizon. What will be required from team members, leaders and organisations if they are to benefit from high performing teams.

# WHY I WROTE THIS BOOK

I've spent my life in and around teams, leadership, learning and performance.

I have worked in Australia and NZ across organisations ranging from my own small business, government agencies, not-for-profit organisations, education through to large corporate organisations. Beyond this, my background includes semi-professional cricket with and against some of the best cricketers in the world in Australia and the UK, as well as marathon running. I bring this passion for teams, leadership, learning and performance to the work that I do.

The clients that I am privileged to work with are similarly diverse. The teams and leaders that I work with range from large banks to construction companies. From iconic online retailers to government procurement departments. From not-for-profit organisation to global consultancy. This allows me to provide insight into organisations, where people's experience is often bound to a particular sector (or even one organisation). I am able to apply the skills and principles honed during my Masters of Business Coaching through Sydney Business School.

I love the work that I do. It is important, meaningful and rewarding. When leaders are able to create environments for higher performing teams, it makes a difference. It leaves a legacy – through the work that the teams do, as well as for the people that grow and flourish when we get it right. I hope that you are reading this because you know that our teams can be better. They can be more flexible, responsive and effective. That there are better ways of using our energy, attention and time than struggling to apply outdated methodologies. I hope that this book gives you some of what you need to make that happen in the teams that you are a part of.

It's a commitment that requires effort, but the reward is significant. Whether you look at it financially, professionally or strategically, team performance is a competitive advantage for leaders and organisations to adopt. The time is now for leaders who can step bravely beyond thinking of teams as simply a unit of resources under command and control to recognising teams as a dynamic collection of people who can be greater than the sum of their parts.

# PART I
# WHAT WAS

The ways that most teams in organisations operate are influenced heavily by what has come before us. If we are to design and implement better ways of operating as teams for now and next, the ability to articulate and understand what has got us here is an advantage. Part I of this book is dedicated to exploring 'what was' for teams. It is not a linear recollection of history, it is an exploration of some of the big influences on your teams today.

We will also take some time to differentiate teams from other ways of getting work done. This is not about semantics, it's about being clear on what teams offer and when they offer the most value. This broader view of teams helps us get a sense of what teams are capable of and how we can use those principles in our time and place.

# CHAPTER 1

# TEAMS AND HUMANITY

**In this chapter we're going to look at:**
- what we can learn from a zebra and a giraffe
- why it can be a good idea to channel Arnold from *Diff'rent Strokes*
- how a nineteenth century industrialist is casting a shadow over twenty-first century organisational structures.

In 2015, my family and I were on holiday in South Africa for a family wedding. We extended the trip (naturally!) and took the opportunity to include a safari. On the recommendation of my uncle, we went to Hluhluwe (pronounced more like Schloo-Schloowee) National Park. It was a life changing experience – as many people who are fortunate enough to see great animals in their natural habitat will tell you.

At Hluhluwe, we were able to drive ourselves in certain areas. One morning we were doing exactly that as a couple of animals decided to walk out in front of us. Out of the bushes arrived a giraffe and his companion – a zebra. We slowed down and simply watched as they went about their morning. They certainly appeared to be very friendly and enjoying each other's company.

When we returned to the accommodation, we spoke to the ranger on duty about what we had witnessed. It turns out that it was no accident or surprise that we saw the giraffe hanging out with the zebra. In fact (and as we saw a lot more during our stay), zebra and giraffe often hang out together. The reason is that they complement each other. Zebra have great hearing, particularly for low range sounds, which means that they are able to detect predators and threats that their giraffe friends cannot. In case it isn't obvious, being tall means that the giraffe are able to see predators and dangers in the distance much better than their striped mates. By working together, they can get more food and decrease their chances of becoming food.

Let's be honest, in Hluhluwe National Park, performance is measured by population numbers. If the number of you and your tribe is stable or increasing over time, you are doing well. If you and your tribe are decreasing in numbers, things aren't so good. In other words, because the zebra and giraffe work together in a way that utilises their complementary capabilities and strengths, they are able to improve their performance.

This behaviour has been shaped by their context. Over thousands of years, their predecessors have discovered, taught, passed on and embedded this way of operating. It is very unlikely that this has required PowerPoint presentations, strategy decks or leadership offsites (would they go to a city for that?).

As we will discover in this book, there is a lot about the way (and the reasons) that the zebra and the giraffe work together that are similar to what we call teams.

# HUMANITY IS BUILT ON TEAMS

The idea of teams or working cooperatively to improve performance is a phenomenon that has served in many settings across nature. Most often, this is within the same species, but as the story of our African friends shows, it can even span across species. Humans are no exception.

If we look around our world, it's clear that we couldn't have achieved what we have on this planet by working as individuals.

Can you imagine how long it would take one person to build an office block? What about to build something like Sydney Harbour Bridge, the Taj Mahal, the pyramids of Giza or the Eiffel Tower? To construct an Airbus A380 aircraft, design a smartphone or tunnel from the UK to mainland Europe? Most of those things would be effectively impossible for an individual – either physically (the labour required would require living longer than we do) or intellectually (one person couldn't know everything that they needed to).

It's not too much of a stretch to say that humanity is built on teams.

Anthropologists and researchers in different fields have come to this same conclusion – even if the words are slightly different. According to a 2006 paper by Steve Kozlowski and Daniel Ilgen of Michigan State University, 'human history is largely a story of people working together in groups to explore, achieve, and conquer'.[1] A similar statement that is often attributed to anthropologist, Margaret Mead (but doesn't seem to appear in any of her published work!) encourages readers to 'never doubt that a small group of thoughtful, committed citizens can change the world; indeed, it's the only thing that ever has'.

# TEAMS ARE BUILT ON HUMANITY

The idea that humanity is built on teams is fairly easy for most of us to acknowledge and accept. What challenges many of the leaders and teams that I work with is that the inverse is also true: teams are built on humanity.

I mean this in two ways. Firstly, our teams are literally made up of people. In the same way that a wall is made of bricks, teams are made of humans. This is an important concept to remind ourselves of, and brings me to my second point. The success of teams is a result of our humanity. The reasons that we can be greater than the sum of our parts and achieve incredible things together is a result of many of the things that make us human – like our ability to communicate, use language and to empathise with others.

# HUMANS, NOT RESOURCES

Resources are things that we use to get tasks done. People are not things, they are wonderfully complex, sentient beings who, (according to behavioural economist Dr Dan Ariely) are predictably irrational.

The inherently irrational nature of humans is exactly why we can't afford treat our teams as a bunch of resources. Resources are consistent, mechanical and excellent at repeating prescribed tasks. Humans are irrational and idiosyncratic. The inconsistency of humans makes us poor as resources (repetitive tasks with little thinking required) and better suited to tasks where there is the need to coordinate, collaborate and overcome challenges that are not able to be solved by following a prescribed set of instructions every time. Resources just do, but don't think – they execute on the instructions given to them. Humans think and do – they execute on the intent and respond to the situation based on their interpretation of the scenario.

To lift the performance of our teams, we need to elevate the humanity in our teams. Treating humans as resources is a way of working that has its roots in the Industrial Revolution of the late nineteenth century. Before we delve into the historical influences on how teams are structured today, let's take a moment to define exactly what I mean by 'team'.

## WHAT A TEAM IS

When you are engaging in work with teams, it's always a good idea to summon the spirit of Gary Coleman and engage your inner Arnold (from *Diff'rent Strokes*) to clarify 'whatchoo talkin' 'bout [colleague]?' This definitely works best if your colleague is named Willis. If you are feeling a little less irreverent or don't have a colleague named Willis, I'd suggest a polite enquiry of 'how are you defining team?' Don't be surprised if the response is vague, unsure or very different from yours (or all of these things).

When it comes to teams, there is no shortage of research, opinions or perspectives. It is less important to decide on a specific 'right' answer than to be clear on the assumptions that each of you are working with. Once you are clear on the assumptions that you are working with, you can test and work with them.

For the purpose of this book I define a team as:

- a small group of people
- with complementary skills

- who are committed to a common purpose, performance goals and approach for which they hold themselves mutually accountable.

This definition might look familiar. It is widely used and has been around for a while. It comes from a 1993 article in *Harvard Business Review* by Jon Katzenbach and Douglas Smith.[2] Despite being almost thirty years old, it has maintained its relevance in the subsequent decades. This definition excludes plenty of groups that many people and organisations (maybe even you and/or your organisation) might call a team. For example, 'a small group of people' means that a large company can't be 'One Team' using this definition. Likewise, people with competing goals or purposes aren't a team. Perhaps most importantly, a group that does not hold each other mutually accountable does not meet the criteria for a team.

When we look at this definition, it's easy to see that in organisational settings:

## All teams are groups, but not all groups are teams.

# WHAT IT TAKES TO BE A TEAM

Perhaps the most important distinction that arises from the definition of team is that it takes a specific way of working for the criteria to be met. It is not enough to throw people together and expect them to hold each other accountable. It is insufficient for people to be drawn together on an organisational chart and assume that they have a common purpose.

These things don't automatically occur. They are the result of work and effort. We'll get to this in more detail later in the book, but for now, it's enough to know that *teams don't become teams simply because you call them one.*

## NINETEENTH CENTURY SHADOW

Many organisations are designed based on beliefs that can be traced back to the nineteenth century, in particular to the work of one man, Frederick Winslow Taylor and his approach of 'scientific management' (sometimes referred to as Taylorism). His work has had a lasting legacy. Taylor analysed how work got done in factories and realised that there were huge gains to be made. His approach was based on his study of a Midvale Steel Company plant in 1881. It led him to an approach based on the assumption that each worker needed to be equipped for their part of the process and that those workers needed to be subsequently monitored closely to ensure that they reduced any waste of resources (including their time and motion). It wasn't too popular with workers when it got implemented to its fullest extent, but business owners seemed to love it. The assumptions held true and led to incredible results. Much more was produced in less time.

You can see the legacy of Taylor's thinking and approaches in the way that many organisations are structured in the 2020s. Most organisations are still based on a series of assumptions that are at least associated with, if not directly linked to, Taylorism. The assumptions that held true and served companies so well include that:

- the work to be done is able to be rationalised to a series of steps or processes
- those processes are able to be well defined, observed and measured through a centralised or hierarchical management structure
- individuals in production roles are readily available and able to be strongly motivated through extrinsic measures such as money or status.

Sound familiar? Almost every organisation – small or large, public or private – applies some of these principles to some extent.

These approaches lead us to reward and recognise particular behaviours and performance. Most reward frameworks are still designed for individual performance and take little or no account of team performance or an individual's contribution to collective performance at team level.

This sends a message about what an organisation believes is important. If we say that teamwork is important and yet our actions reward individual performance, the message that is most likely to be received is that people in our organisation should prioritise individual performance over collaboration. If we say that culture matters, but we promote what Netflix call 'brilliant jerks' who are technically excellent and interpersonally dysfunctional – we send a signal that such behaviour is not only acceptable but rewarded.

The result of this is that we are setting ourselves to swim against the tide. We want more collaborative and high performing teams for the 2020s and beyond, and yet:

- our teams are structured based on outdated assumptions
- our reward frameworks promote individualistic and not collective performance.

The way that we see teams in organisations needs to evolve. Taylor's view of teams places the greatest emphasis on each component (either the person or process) and very little on the connections or spaces between the components in a team. A hallmark of teams (not groups) is that they are greater than the sum of their parts. Following that logic, simply focusing on the parts can't be enough to achieve great team performance.

## RECAP

## HUMANITY IS BUILT ON TEAMS AND TEAMS ARE BUILT ON HUMANITY

Teams have been a part of humanity across time, cultures and contexts. They are a core reason that we have been able to achieve so much on this planet in so many different settings.

Humanity is the reason that teams work. Our ability to elevate the humanity within our teams means that we can maximise the benefits of teams for our organisations at the same time as making it a rewarding experience for team members.

The word 'team' is used liberally in modern settings. This muddies the waters and leads us to treating all groups as teams, when this is not the case. Clarity on what a team is (and isn't) allows us to take actions that support team performance. We need to understand some of the assumptions underpinning the way that teams are structured and operate in order to design and implement better ways of working for now and next.

## REVIEW QUESTIONS

Use these questions to capture your own thoughts or facilitate a conversation with your team.

### TEAMS AND HUMANITY

- What would not exist if humans didn't have the ability to work as teams?
- How well does your team connect with each other as humans (not resources)?
- What are some things that make humans feel like resources?

### DEFINING TEAMS

- How do you define a team?
- Do you agree that not all groups are teams?
- What teams are you a part of (both work and non-work)?

### OPERATING AS A TEAM

- What assumptions do you have about how teams operate?
- What has worked in the past and is likely to continue to serve teams moving into the future?
- What has worked in the past but is no longer serving teams?

## ACTIVITY – TEAM TIME CAPSULE

Each chapter includes a quick exercise that you can run either by yourself or with your teams. This chapter's exercise is the team time capsule.

What is a
team?

Teams

What is required for a
high performing team?

### PURPOSE

Use this activity as a way of:

- individuals articulating their current perspectives on teams and team performance
- facilitating a conversation about that
- assessing any changes in perspectives of team performance over time.

### WHAT YOU'LL NEED

- A4 paper and marker
- 3+ people – larger groups may be best split into smaller groups up to 10

## DEGREE OF DIFFICULTY
Easy – requires few resources and basic facilitation skills

## INSTRUCTIONS

### STEP 1
Each participant captures their answers to the following question in a mind map:
- What is a team?
- What is required for a high performing team?

### STEP 2
If sharing as a whole group, facilitate a conversation around:
- What was common among the group?
- What were some surprises?
- What are the implications of this?

Ask participants to share what they have written with others. Do this in pairs, small groups or as a whole group as required.

### STEP 3
Repeat the exercise at another time (I recommend at least three months away) and have participants compare and contrast their individual and collective responses.
- Add additional questions to the group debrief of:
- What (if anything) has changed?
- What do you attribute that change (or consistency) to?
- Collect each participant's response anc keep in a safe place.

# CHAPTER 2

# WHAT IS REQUIRED

**In this chapter we are going to:**
- **question some popular twentieth century thinking about teams**
- **compare teams with telephones**
- **reimagine the acronym VUCA.**

Imagine that the date is 24 February, 1998 (or any time in 1998 will be fine!). You are planning on meeting a friend for lunch and a drink. They live on the other side of the city, so it's best to meet somewhere about the same travel time for each of you. How would you do it? Chances are that you would probably have to:
- call them on the phone (probably a landline, but possibly an analogue mobile phone) to arrange a time and place
- get out the Yellow Pages to find a place if neither of you knew one that was about half-way
- set a specific time and place to meet them.

When it came time to travel, you would head into the car and open up your street directory (maybe keeping it on your lap as you got close). You'd get to the pub and have to decide if you'd sit in the smoking or non-smoking section.

It's only two decades, but for someone who is born after 2005, this would seem like it was a century ago! Why not send them a text? Why didn't you Google a restaurant for the area? What do you mean street directory, there was no GPS? In fact, why not just get an Uber so you can have a few drinks? You could smoke inside pubs?

The world is changing fast and the way we work, live, travel and function is vastly different from not that long ago. Much of that is due to the rapid development of technology, but there are also changes in what we expect of each other – and the services that we use.

This chapter is going to look at some more recent changes and their impacts on team performance. It is important for us to appreciate the rate of change in the current operating environment so that our teams are set up for what is, rather than what was.

## TWENTIETH CENTURY THINKING

It's not just Taylor's nineteenth century view casting a shadow, there's also some twentieth century thinking about team performance that we are holding on to.

From around the mid-1960s, it was typical to view teams through the lens of Input-Process-Output. It was around that time that Bruce Tuckman's popular model (Forming, Norming, Storming, Performing) gained prominence. It was a model reflective of its time. Interestingly, in 1977, Tuckman, along with

Mary Ann Jensen, added a fifth stage: adjourning, that involves completing the task and breaking up the team.

For a long while this and other similar models seemed to work well for team performance. It's likely that you have heard this phrase or seen it referred to. It remains popular for a few reasons. It has high face validity (it makes sense at a glance), it rhymes (which makes it easy to remember) and it's popular (ironically, much like a busy restaurant attracts more customers, a popular model gains its own momentum as more people use it!). It has numerous limitations, including some acknowledged by Tuckman himself, who said 'what has been presented is mainly research dealing with sequential development observed in therapy groups'.[1] It is worth questioning how relevant that is for your teams in the 2020s.

## BEYOND 2000

Around the turn of this century, there was a sense that Tuckman and other similar models didn't quite capture the essence of how teams were operating. The way that teams were seen was considered largely through a lens of Input – Mediating Factors (that included but weren't limited to team processes) – Output. In terms of applied models across organisations, a very widely applied one came from Patrick Lencioni's *The Five Dysfunctions of a Team*.[2] That book presents a model that identifies a sequence of dysfunctions (or in more academic terms 'mediating factors') that inhibit team performance.

The book and the model are very popular and widely applied. Like most of Lencioni's books, the bulk of it is written as a business fable and doesn't claim to be based on a lot of peer reviewed evidence. Once again, it is a model that has benefited many teams and organisations and is reflective of its time. As we have already discussed, though – our world is rapidly changing.

## THE TEAMS, THEY ARE A-CHANGING

Here are a few of the key ways in which teams in organisations have shifted in this century alone:

## FROM CLEAR BOUNDARIES TO FLUID

Teams were typically seen as well defined and distinct units that had distinct membership that was easily identifiable. Now, up to 95% of knowledge workers are on more than one team at work and it's not uncommon for individuals to be a part of a dozen separate teams professionally.[3]

## FROM STABLE TO RAPIDLY CHANGING

Being a part of many teams felt like a High Court appointment – the members remained the same until they retired or died! Now, it is common for the team members to change rapidly as average tenure in organisations reduces as well as the skills required for different phases of work change.

## FROM GEOGRAPHICALLY CO-LOCATED TO PARTIALLY OR FULLY REMOTE

No longer do teams need to be in the same place at the same time. While it is difficult to operate a factory or production line remotely, there are many teams that do most of their work either partially or fully remotely. The physical distancing and movement restrictions brought about in response to the COVID-19 pandemic highlighted to many people just what was possible without a physical hub.

### FROM FUNCTIONALLY DISTINCT TO DISTINCTLY CROSS-FUNCTIONAL

In line with the view that the independent parts are more important for performance at team level, many organisations held the belief that maximising the performance of each part of their operation (sales, production, marketing, administration, etc) was more important than how those parts interacted. What is evident now is that there are more collaborative ways of working at all levels of organisations with cross-functional teams increasingly chosen as the way to achieve objectives.

### FROM FORMALLY DEFINED TO INFORMAL ALLIANCES

It used to be easy to identify teams by looking at an organisational chart. A report released by the ADP Research Institute in 2019[4] suggests that about half of the work done in organisations is through teams that are not captured in the company's formal structure.

# USING A 2G PHONE ON A 5G NETWORK

Teams that are increasingly diverse in every aspect (composition, location, function and so on) can't rely on frameworks that assume team development and performance is linear, predictable and controllable. It may be uncomfortable, but it's the truth. It's debatable about whether teams were ever really linear or static. It was sufficient in days gone by to think about teams in that way. Those days are behind us and we need a way to see teams as the complex, dynamic and human systems that they are.

To ram home this point, I'd like you to consider telephones. Yes, telephones. Think about the structure, capability and functionality of phones in each of these eras:

- 1960s – circa Tuckman's Forming, Storming, Norming, Performing model
  Telephones were fixed to walls, landline only, analogue and only transmitted voice
- Early 2000s – circa Lencioni's Five Dysfunctions Model
  Telephones were increasingly mobile, able to send voice and data (mainly SMS) on monochromatic screens
- 2020s
  Telephones are almost exclusively mobile, transmit high volumes of data, have high resolution cameras and screens and, as you may have heard previously, each phone contains more computing power than NASA used to send Neil Armstrong and co to the moon.

There are parallels that we can draw between the development of telephones and what our teams need to succeed. As telephones have developed, it has not been a matter of discarding everything that we know to date and starting afresh. What happened is that useful features are retained in the next generation, and what is not useful is either discarded, replaced or upgraded. For your teams to be successful, you can't simply accept that they will operate as they have done previously. We need to critically assess what is required of us and ask ourselves:

- What has worked in the past and is likely to continue to serve us moving into the future?
- What has worked in the past but is no longer serving us?
- What do we need to adjust to perform better in current conditions?
  You wouldn't even try to use a phone from the early 2000s

to perform tasks that you need to do on a 5G network. It sounds ridiculous...and yet, too many of us are applying principles from those times (or earlier) with our teams and expecting them to succeed in a very different world.

## VUCA NEEDS VUCA

You may be familiar with the acronym VUCA. It stands for volatile, uncertain, complex and ambiguous. The term has been around for over 30 years and was popularised in military circles in the early 2000s.

It's hard to deny that the world we live in is a VUCA place. We need only to consider the COVID-19 epidemic and the impacts of that to see how rapidly the world can change in profound ways. Within a space of weeks, countries went from operating 'as normal' to almost every aspect of society changing. Our movements were restricted – initially with international travel before rapidly getting to the point where billions of people across the globe were instructed to stay home. Businesses saw their cashflow stop overnight. Globally, millions of people lost their job and were faced with the implications of that. Trillions of dollars were spent by governments across the world in response to mitigate the health, societal and economic impacts of this virus. It is likely that the impact will be felt for years or decades to come.

Our world is changing at an unprecedented rate with technological, societal and political changes providing plenty of things that leaders need to respond to daily. This has implications for all of us and the teams that we are a part of. The rate of change means that something that has been effective for years, decades or centuries can become obsolete overnight. This means that all of us hoping to be more effective need to adjust our way of working – both individually and collectively.

In a leadership development program a few years ago, I was talking to the group about the idea of VUCA. Over lunch, I was thinking about what this meant for how the best leaders and teams respond to the VUCA world. What I came up with was unscientific, but seemed useful. Here it is for your consideration – **VUCA needs VUCA**.

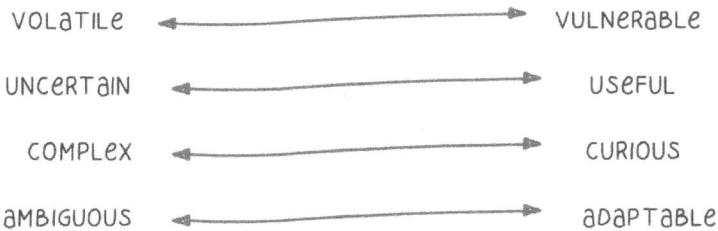

| VOLATILE | ⟷ | VULNERABLE |
| UNCERTAIN | ⟷ | USEFUL |
| COMPLEX | ⟷ | CURIOUS |
| AMBIGUOUS | ⟷ | ADAPTABLE |

*A way of reimagining the acronym VUCA for our teams.*

## VOLATILE NEEDS VULNERABLE

The rapid and unpredictable nature of changes that we are experiencing challenges us from knowing what the 'right' answer is. We are in situations that are without precedent so we can't rely fully on history to guide us. The fact that there may not be *one* right answer (there may be none or there may be many) means that we need to open ourselves up to more possibilities and let go of being the expert. Questions become more powerful than answers.

## UNCERTAIN NEEDS USEFUL

Because we are grappling with the idea that there may not be one right answer, trying to be right can feel a little like nailing jelly to the wall. Difficult and not likely to last very long even if you somehow manage it! Aiming for utility is a more productive use of our energy, attention and time. This is not to excuse behaviour that is purely short term. Quite often being useful in a VUCA world means being able to see the bigger picture – taking the longer, slower road that leads further.

## COMPLEX NEEDS CURIOUS

A hallmark of complexity is that there is not a linear relationship between cause and effect. What we need is to be able to view the whole system (or systems) that we are operating in, notice patterns and run experiments. Developing a genuine interest in what is happening is an essential skill for a VUCA world. The best tool at our disposal for this is to develop our appetite and capacity for reflection.

## AMBIGUOUS NEEDS ADAPTABLE

It seems obvious that to operate in a world that is changing fast, those that can change fast will be at an advantage. Hierarchical and process driven ways of working struggle to respond quickly enough and often find themselves continuously one (or many) steps behind where they need to be. What we will see in this book is that those operating as real teams are resilient in the face of change.

# GETTING WORK DONE IN A VUCA WORLD

As you are reading, there is probably little doubt in your mind that I believe that teams and teamwork are important to success in the 2020s. What may be less obvious is that it is important to acknowledge that teams are *not* always the answer. There are times when the task at hand may be better suited to independent or leader dependent work. One of the most powerful conversations I have with clients is how to differentiate between different ways that work can get done.

Below is a quick overview of three ways of working – as individuals, as a group and as a team. These types of working are better suited to different operating environments and provide different benefits.

### INDIVIDUALS

Work that requires no interaction with others. It's ideal for what Cal Newport calls Deep Work – 'the ability to focus without distraction on a cognitively demanding task' – assuming that the individual has all of the capability that they require to do that work.

### GROUP

Work that requires a number of people to follow specific instructions or procedures. To do, *not* think. The leader has visibility and responsibility for all of the work that the team does.

### TEAM

Work that requires interdependence to be greater than the sum of their parts. The leader's responsibility is to empower and enable team members, who need to think *and* do.

Let's briefly look into how each way of working is distinct. In workshops, teams come up with their own way of differentiating between individuals, groups and teams. There are probably 50+ different ways that I have seen teams look at this. What is included here are the most common and pertinent ones to keep in mind as we look to lift the performance of teams.

# HOW MUCH FLEX DO YOU NEED?

We have spoken of how fast and significant many changes in the world are. It makes sense to consider how each way of working responds to changes in context.

### INDIVIDUALS

Working solo is a double-edged sword. It makes us both *agile and fragile*. As individuals, we are agile as we can shift quickly and be highly responsive to changes in the environment. It also makes us vulnerable to some external factors – like getting sick.

### GROUP

This way of working is perfect – until it's not! By design, groups work wonderfully and are *robust* within clearly defined parameters. When they are stretched beyond the limitations of their design, their effectiveness falls away very quickly like the proverbial fish out of water.

## TEAM

The inherent qualities of true teamwork provide *resilience*. Teams possess an ability to be responsive and adaptable to changes in context. Teams can access the shared capabilities and complementary strengths to work towards their shared purpose.

Operational flexibility is both a feature and benefit of teams. Teams that function with more adaptable and resilient approaches are more likely to fit the definition of a team (and are not a team by name only). Also, this adaptability is one of the reasons that teams are so useful, especially in a fast-paced operating environment.

# WHEN ALL YOU'VE GOT IS A HAMMER...

I have already stated that teams are not always the answer for the problems that we are faced with. Importantly, though, the ability to operate as a team provides access to each way of working. By that I mean that if you can operate as a team, you are also able to choose when you operate in a more leader-dependent way or when it may be better for members to work individually. The inverse is also true.

If you are only able to operate as an individual, you will be limited in the amount of work that you can produce. In most scenarios, more people working together (even ineffectively) will deliver greater quantity of work than one individual.

The capability to only work as a group (and not as a team) is likely to see leaders and organisations attempt to force complex environments through the lens of a complicated paradigm that can be fixed through rules, processes and procedures. It is here where most leaders, teams and organisations find themselves. For reasons that we have explored it is difficult to move beyond this – and almost impossible without making a concerted and coordinated effort.

One of the great benefits of the ability to operate as a team is allowing conscious choice of how work gets done – and to match that with what the situation dictates.

## WHAT'S REQUIRED HERE?

Some of the wisest advice and questions have simplicity that belie their depth. Dr Gordon Spence was the Course Director of my Masters of Business Coaching Program. Very early on during the program, he shared with us a question that he keeps in mind during coaching. As part of your teams, it's one that I encourage you to keep in mind...*What's required here?*

It seems so simple and so obvious and yet it is the essence of operating best in teams.

At one end of the spectrum, asking 'what's required here' can help you to consider what is necessary in the context of organisational, national or global systems. It can help you to consider what is being asked of your teams in the context of this point in history as technology and society make shifts that we haven't seen before.

At the other end of the spectrum, asking 'what's required here' can help you to consider what is the best use of your energy, attention and time at this very moment. Do you need to send an email or pick up the phone? Do you need to focus on the task or the people? What does your team need from you at this time?

Somewhere in the middle lies the question of 'what's required here – for us to work as individuals, a group or a team?'. Making that decision consciously and consistently can drive the right behaviours for the context that you are operating in.

## RECAP

# WHAT WAS REQUIRED IS NOT WHAT IS REQUIRED

What was required in organisations since the times of Taylor has been group work. Tightly controlled, managed and supervised operation of well understood and defined processes. What is required now is operating as a team. In a way that is flexible, resilient and responsive to the environment that we are operating in.

As the world shifts rapidly, it is becoming less likely that any one of us has the answer to every question that we face. Individual subject matter expertise or experience is deep, but narrow and it means that any one person can run into the limits of their ability to make a meaningful difference alone. We need to be able to harness collective intelligence and capability that is better able to identify and respond to a fast moving operating environment.

That will require each of us to adapt the ways that we get work done. The good news is that if you are reading this book and are prepared to embark upon a course of action that improves the performance of the teams that you work with and for, you are at a distinct advantage

In Part II of the book, we will explore the Team Performance System that will allow you to observe teams in a more dynamic way in order to maximise the benefits of teams for the 2020s.

## REVIEW QUESTIONS

Use these questions to capture your own thoughts or facilitate a conversation with your team.

### RATE OF CHANGE

- What has become outdated in the past 5, 10 or 20 years? Consider things both inside and outside of work.
- What exists in the world now that would amaze a version of yourself from 20 years ago?
- How do you keep yourself up to date with the outside world?

### VUCA NEEDS VUCA

- What will it take for you to be more *vulnerable*?
- Can you shift your mindset to being *useful* rather than being right?
- How can you cultivate a sense of *curiosity* in yourself and others?
- When was the last time you were able to be *adaptable*?

### WAYS OF WORKING

- What are situations where operating as a team is valuable?
- When is operating as a team not as effective as individual or group work?
- Can you build the agility in your team that allows both team and individual work?

# ACTIVITY – WAYS OF WORKING

| STRUCTURE | WAY OF WORKING | SUITED TO | PERFORMANCE | ADAPTABILITY |
|---|---|---|---|---|
| TEAM | INTERDEPENDENT | | | |
| GROUP | LEADER DEPENDENT | | | |
| INDIVIDUALS | SELF-DEPENDENT | | | |

## PURPOSE

Use this activity as a way of:

- differentiating ways of working – individual, group and team
- highlighting the behavioural differences between groups and teams
- facilitating a conversation about when each way of working is useful.

## WHAT YOU'LL NEED

- whiteboard or flip chart
- markers for whiteboard or flip chart
- 3+ people (larger groups are best split into groups of up to 10)
- 45 – 60 minutes

## INSTRUCTIONS

### STEP 1
Draw or construct a grid of 4 rows and at least 5 columns and label as per image.

### STEP 2
Begin leading the conversation by completing the first row using the terms:
- Self-dependent
- Leader Dependent
- Interdependent

    Talk through each as you go.

    This will give participants a sense of what will be required of them.

### STEP 3
Ask the group to give their perspectives on each of the rows in order.

*Note: As a facilitator, your role is to summarise the responses from the room. You may need to guide this if people are unsure at various stages.*

### STEP 4
Use the blank row for any dimension that the group feels is relevant. Some suggestions include:
- Leadership
- Decision Making
- Diversity of Thought
- Response to Conflict

Ask participants to share what they have written with others. Do this in pairs, small groups or as a whole group as required. If sharing as a whole group, facilitate a conversation around:

- What was common among the group?
- What were some surprises?
- What are the implications of this?

**STEP 5**

Facilitate a conversation around:

- What are the implications of this for the team?
- What are the implications of this for each team member?

# PART II

# WHAT IS

I had the opportunity to work with a procurement team in a local health district in late 2019. They were expected to deliver significant tangible value (savings) for their district over the coming months, but were lacking a deliberate approach to working together to achieve this. Over the course of a few months, we worked our way through the principles of the Team Performance System in a series of workshops.

In March 2020, shoppers were hoarding toilet paper, hand sanitiser was a status symbol and supermarket shelves were empty. The general public in Australia was anxious, stressed and overwhelmed by a situation most of us could not have imagined. While this was happening, I reached out to the procurement team leader to check in. Given that procurement was a struggle for households, I anticipated that it was a challenging time for procurement in hospitals.

Below is an edited copy and paste of our exchange:

I asked her...

*How are you and the team doing? Been thinking of you – must be an incredibly busy and challenging time for you all. It's hard enough for most of us in the general public, but this pandemic must be putting incredible pressure on procurement and across health.*

Here is how she responded...

*We are under the pump but organised, productive and really adaptable to everything that comes our way. I couldn't be prouder of this team right now!!! I think we are starting to change thinking because we know what we are doing – how cool is that!*

I wasn't expecting it, but that's what she said – a very pleasant surprise. This reflects what can happen when teams do the work on themselves and for themselves. It reflects the value of real teamwork, of creating an environment that allows individuals to work together on important work and how this becomes evident to others outside of the team.

The same applies for your teams. Taking a deliberate approach to team performance will serve you now and into the future. The sooner, the better.

The first step is to be able to see teams as they are. This section of the book will help you do that. We'll be looking at how teams work through the lens of the Team Performance System.

What is the Team Performance System? It's a way to view what is happening within teams. It will show you

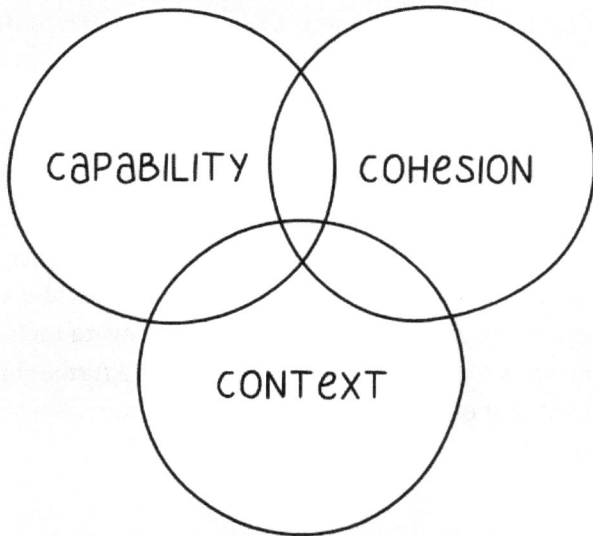

that a team's performance is the product of its capability, cohesion and context.

- Capability: The ability of team members to perform tasks.
- Cohesion: How well team members can work together to perform tasks.
- Context: The circumstances and setting for the team.
  Most people looking to improve team performance spend their energy on capability or cohesion. When it is about capability, they say things like 'we need to get more people in' or 'we need a different skillset in our team', which can either be developed within current members or by adding new members. When it is about cohesion, you will hear things like 'they are very talented, but don't play well

together' or 'they are all working hard but pulling in different directions'. There is no doubt that these are important elements that impact the performance of any team and are worth paying attention to. But there's one more vital piece of the puzzle: context. Context is the hidden foundation to great teams.

In Part II we'll be looking at how understanding each of these dimensions of the Team Performance System will help you to bring people together and elevate their performance. But first we need to look a little further into a concept that underpins the Team Performance System: complexity.

# CHAPTER 3

# COMPLEXITY

In this chapter, we are going to look at:
* why teams are not 'complicated'
* the complex relationship between complexity and teams
* how teams are like a loaf of bread.

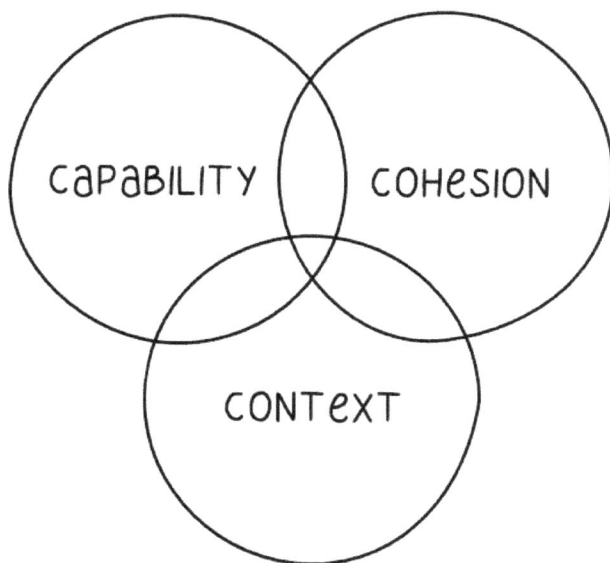

In my early 20s, I had a short backpacking holiday in Italy. I was in Florence and wanted to get to Rome. As you might expect, I was watching my Euros and keen to make my limited money stretch. My plan was to use a classic backpacker move – get the overnight bus. In case it's not immediately apparent, that means that you get both travel and accommodation sorted in one transaction. It's basically a free night of accommodation. Genius.

To put my plan into action, I headed to the bus station. I spoke to the woman at one window, who told me that there were no buses – only trains. I concluded that given the language barrier (my non-existent Italian and English as her second language) that it must have been a linguistic issue. I went around the corner to another bus company. Same issue.

After the third conversation, I realised that maybe there were no buses. How could that be? Everyone knows that all roads lead to Rome!

The problem here was that I was operating based on a number of assumptions that were incorrect and insufficient for what was required. I stuck at my intended plan for too long and didn't respond to what was actually happening. I rationalised my errors as something lost in translation between me and the attendants. In hindsight, it's obvious that the error was mine – specifically the way that I was looking at the situation.

We can do the same sort of thing with teams. If we are dogmatic in our assumptions about how teams should work, hold onto outdated or erroneous assumptions, we can fail to see what is actually happening or we can jump to incorrect conclusions.

To see teams as they are, rather than how we think they should be, the first thing we need to look at is the concept of complexity and how it relates to teams.

# TEAMS AREN'T COMPLICATED – THEY'RE COMPLEX

We have already touched on the concept of VUCA in Chapter 2. Within the four elements of VUCA, it is the concept of complexity that is central to operating in teams. Working with teams and leaders, there is always one model that sits in the back of my head. It's called the Cynefin model and was introduced by David Snowden when he was working at IBM.[1] While I find it hard to pronounce (my Welsh is pretty much non-existent), it is incredibly influential in the way that we are able to look at ourselves and our teams. Basically, the Cynefin model talks about different types of systems:

## 1. SIMPLE

This is where systems have a linear connection between cause and effect, such as operating a light switch. With high predictability and immediately observable results you can see what happens if you turn the light switch on or off.

## 2. COMPLICATED

This is a series of connected simple systems. Even something as technically challenging as a jet engine might be considered complicated. It is possible (for people much smarter than me), to understand how each part interacts and the link between cause and effect (even with lots of links in the chain).

## 3. COMPLEX

In complexity, there is not a linear relationship between cause and effect. The best example that I can think of is the weather, which is incredibly complex. Meteorologists make remarkably accurate predictions on most days by using modelling based on current and historical patterns. They occasionally get it wrong simply because we cannot know exactly how all of the parts of the weather system will interact.

## 4. CHAOS

In chaotic systems there is no apparent connection between cause and effect. This feels to me like dealing with a toddler in the middle of a tantrum! Our adult minds typically cannot understand why they are upset or what will make them more or less upset. The toddler probably doesn't know, either.

I am not an expert in complexity or systems thinking. You can Google some more for yourself – be warned, it could lead you down a few rabbit holes! I know enough to know that I have much more to learn. It is sufficient for this framework to be held in our minds as a useful reminder. In particular, it is valuable to distinguish complicated from complex.

You and I, as humans, are complex systems. We are unpredictable and there is no way that anyone can 100% guarantee that our actions will be exactly the same – even in response to the same or similar stimulus. We know that within ourselves. So, what happens when we ask a group of complex humans to work together? Of course, it's complex. Throw into that mix that we are working with other complex teams in complex and fast moving environments and you can see that we are operating in layers of complexity and perhaps moving towards the edge of chaos.

OK, so what's the point? It's this:

**One of the hallmarks of complex systems is that, by definition, the same action may lead to different results.**

There are some causal relationships that seem clearer in hindsight (hence the value of reflection), but there aren't guarantees of exact replication.

This is an uncomfortable, but important concept for us to grapple with in our teams. In complex environments, where cause and effect aren't linear and repeatable, we can't have real certainty. There might not be a right answer or a right way. Sometimes there are many 'right' answers – other times there are none.

This is the reason that teams in the 2020s need to be able to learn, adapt and respond to their present context as opposed to being governed by the processes and structures of times gone by. And this is why complexity is the underpinning principle of the Team Performance System.

## EMBRACING COMPLEXITY

We need to embrace complexity in order to see *what is* happening for our current teams and operate effectively within them. If we don't we are likely to:

- fail to see the potential influences and forces on our teams
- misinterpret situations as we look for a linear cause and effect relationship
- take overly simplistic reactive measures rather than considered responsive approaches to challenges in our teams.

Embracing complexity was the central theme of a 2019 academic paper reviewing the previous decade of team research. That paper looked at literally hundreds of studies either directly or through meta-analyses. The title gives a sense of the authors' views on the importance of complexity in being able to truly appreciate teams in 2020 – *Embracing Complexity: Reviewing the Past Decade of Team Effectiveness Research.*[2]

In case there was any doubt, the opening page of the paper includes the line that in order to see teams, we can *'benefit from a conceptualisation of them as dynamic networks and modelling them as small complex systems'.*

It is clear. One of the best things that we can do to appreciate what is happening in our teams is to accept the principles of complexity.

## COMPLEXITY NEEDS TEAMS

In Chapter 1 I talked about how humanity is built on teams and teams are built on humanity. We can look at complexity the same way – teams are complex and complexity needs teams.

We know that as the world shifts rapidly, it is becoming less likely that any one of us has the answer to every question that we face. Our subject matter expertise or experience is deep, but narrow. Alone we can quickly run into the limits of its ability to influence meaningfully. The demands on our work mean that if we want to make a significant positive difference, we need to be able to harness collective intelligence and capability.

In 2013, EY surveyed 821 executives from 14 countries to find out their views on whether teams are useful in addressing complex challenges that they faced.[3]

## 89% of respondents agree that the problems confronting them are now so complex that teams are essential to provide effective solutions.

Just as importantly, 82% of respondents agree that improving their organisation's ability to develop and manage teams will be essential for future competitiveness.

It's not just EY who found this. A 2019 report from another global consultancy, Deloitte,[4] calls organisational performance a 'team sport'. In other words, the competitiveness of organisations in the current and emerging climate relies on the ability to operate in teams. The Deloitte research picked up some interesting trends – in particular, the gap between the opportunity presented by working through teams and the current reality. The shift from 'functional hierarchy to team-centric and network-based organisational models' was viewed as important or very important by 65% of the survey respondents — but only 7% felt very ready to execute this shift.

Bringing these threads together, there is a strong correlation between the Cynefin framework and the classification of ways of working that we looked at in Chapter 2.

### INDIVIDUALS – SIMPLE
Individual work is best suited to simple environments, where there are very few variables and those that exist are readily able to be predicted and controlled.

### GROUP – COMPLICATED
Group work is best suited to complicated environments where there are many variables, but experienced leaders are able to confidently predict and control the work that needs to be done.

### TEAM – COMPLEX

Teams are best suited in complex environments with increasing speed of change and decreasing predictability.

One nuance worth noting is around individual work. Individual work is a structure can be well suited for complex *tasks* in a simple *environment* of isolation where one person is not required to coordinate with others. An example of this is the deep thinking that many knowledge workers are requ red to do – they may benefit from turning off their phone and email alerts and being decidedly uncollaborative at various points. What is likely, though, is that they will intersperse these periods of individual work with times where they reconnect with colleagues in order to test and stretch their thinking (in other words, as a team).

# TEAMS ARE EMERGENT

The concept of emergence is central to both teams and complexity. Something is emergent when it somehow becomes greater than (or at least different to) the sum of its parts. This might be sounding vague, so here is an example to illustrate.

Bread is emergent. The ingredients – the flour, the water, the salt and so on – are not bread. None of them by themselves is bread. Even simply bringing them together doesn't make bread. Once those same ingredients are combined in the right ratios and put through a process (in this instance baking), they become something different (and I reckon much better) than the separate parts or even the sum of the parts.

For teams, this is our aspiration.

We want people to be better together and do more meaningful

work than they could possibly do without each other. If not, what is the point in being a team? We would be better off working independently or without any interaction between members. A belief and awareness of emergence helps us to take a deliberate approach to team performance.

# WORKING WITH COMPLEXITY

It is essential for us to appreciate the importance of complexity. It is central to understanding the performance of our teams. We simply cannot know with 100% confidence what is going to happen for any given team at any given time. Here are a few tips to help you better navigate the complexity of your teams.

## PRINCIPLES VS. RULES

Finish this sentence... 'Rules are made to be _____'. Most people will respond with 'broken'. This is a clue for why rules may not be as useful as we think in complex environments.

The goal of rules is control and compliance that ensures that team members follow instructions prescribed by the leader and/or organisation. The success of rules relies on some risky assumptions – that conditions are stable or predictable, that a given action will always lead to the same outcome and that those in positions of authority know more than others. And as we've established, this is not the case in our complex workplaces and fast-paced times.

When we set up rules, we set up the potential for a power struggle. We will have team members who will find themselves railing against rules that they perceive as unfair, restrictive or unreasonable. They will do what they can to work around the rules as leaders are doing their best to ensure that those people play by the rules. On the flip side, we have people who are drawn to following those rules and feel very comfortable and safe within the confines of the rules. Neither of these are great outcomes.

While rules are meant to be broken, principles are intended to be guidelines. They are based on assumptions, reflections and experience (as are rules). The big difference with principles is that they acknowledge that in complex environments it is not possible to have a rule for every situation that may present itself.

## The goal of principles is to empower team members to make decisions and take actions that they can be confident are in the best interest of the team.

For the parts of a team's work that are definitely repeatable and controllable, it makes sense to have rules – monthly reports, timesheets and so on. But for work that has more moving parts, variety and unpredictability because they are without an exact precedent, principles will serve you and your team better. Principles are more responsive, adaptable and far better suited to the complex environments that our teams operate in.

## EFFECTIVENESS VS. EFFICIENCY

One of the secrets of great teams it that they prioritise effectiveness over efficiency. It may sound like the same thing or that it's just semantics, but just like the difference between complicated and complex, there is a stark difference. I'll explain with a clear distinction:

- Prioritising efficiency focuses on improving processes.
- Prioritising effectiveness focuses on improving outcomes.

## In complex environments, effective beats efficient every time.

While great teams strive for both efficiency and effectiveness, they make a deliberate choice to prioritise effectiveness. Often, improving efficiency can lead to increased effectiveness. As long as efficiency gains are aligned with improving effectiveness, that's great.

Because we are operating in environments where it's simply not possible to control all of the variables that impact our work, we can run into problems when efficiency and effectiveness are competing. In a business setting, this could be a call centre aiming to reduce their average handling time (efficiency) rather than increasing customer outcomes like satisfaction or resolution (effectiveness). It's clear here that the improvement in efficiency at the expense of effectiveness will not benefit the business or the customers.

When we try to reduce our team's way of working into a set of rationalised and prescribed interactions, we will inevitably reduce the ability of the team to perform at their best collectively. In this environment straining for control and striving for ever more efficient processes is the wrong goal. Your teams *might* need to be more efficient. What's more likely is that your team needs to be more effective.

## COMPLEXITY IS AT THE HEART OF TEAM PERFORMANCE

Complexity is a principle that allows us to operate with teams as they are, not as they were or as we want them to be. Through this chapter, we have looked at the distinction between complicated and complex, rules and principles, and efficient and effective.

The table below summarises the benefits of team performance that have already been mentioned with particular reference to complexity. This is just a small sample of my version of the exercise in Chapter 2.

| STRUCTURE | WAY OF WORKING | SUITED TO | PERFORMANCE | ADAPTABILITY |
|---|---|---|---|---|
| TEAM | INTERDEPENDENT | COMPLEX ENVIRONMENTS | EFFECTIVE | RESILIENT |
| GROUP | LEADER DEPENDENT | COMPLICATED ENVIRONMENTS | EFFICIENT | ROBUST |
| INDIVIDUALS | SELF-DEPENDENT | SIMPLE ENVIRONMENTS | INEFFECTIVE | FRAGILE |

*Differentiating ways of working – individual, group and team*

In a nutshell, teams offer a way of working that is suited to complex environments by being more responsive and tapping into the collective capabilities of its members. The ability to team up is a distinct competitive advantage for leaders and organisations.

# REVIEW QUESTIONS

Use these questions to capture your own thoughts or facilitate a conversation with your team.

## SYSTEMS
What elements of your work are:
- simple – with a linear relationship between cause and effect?
- complicated – a series of connected simple systems?
- complex – where there is not a linear relationship between cause and effect?

## DISTINCTIONS
- How would you describe the distinction between complicated and complex?
- How would you describe the distinction between rules and principles?
- How would you describe the distinction between efficient and effective?

## EMBRACING COMPLEXITY
- Do you see complexity play out in the teams that you are a part of?
- How can your teams become more comfortable operating in complexity?
- When might complexity be an advantage for your teams?

## ACTIVITY – VISUAL TELEGRAM

First statement

Then some more words are added

The last words are here

## PURPOSE

Use this activity as a way of:

- demonstrating the importance of sharing information
- engaging the group with an activity that exposes them to ambiguity
- facilitating a conversation about how to better communicate within teams.

## WHAT YOU'LL NEED

- one sheet of A4 paper per participant
- pens/markers for participants
- 5+ people
- 15 – 30 minutes

## INSTRUCTIONS

### STEP 1

Ask participants to write a short, simple statement in the top fifth of the page (see image). A prompt may include 'What is something that you have done today or this week?'

### STEP 2

Once the statement is completed, each participant passes their sheet to the person next to them. Now ask each participant to represent the statement visually on the next fifth of the page.

Pictionary rules apply!

- no letters
- no numbers
- no symbols.

## STEP 3

Participants fold the paper back so that the writing is no longer visible and only the image is visible. Once this is done, it is passed to the person next to them (same direction). Each participant then writes a statement that captures the image that is visible to them in words on the next fifth of the page.

## STEP 4

Participants fold the paper back so that only the writing is visible. With the new sheet, each participant represents the statement visually on the next fifth of the page. Pictionary rules still apply.

## STEP 5

Participants fold the paper back so that only the image is visible. Once this is done, it is passed to the person next to them (same direction). Each participant then writes a statement that captures the image that is visible to them in words on the next fifth of the page.

## STEP 6

Return folded sheets to original writer. This should require passing the sheet in the opposite direction four times. Once each participant has their original sheet returned to them, ask them to unfold the paper and compare the first and last statements.
- Were any close?
- Were any wildly different?

Facilitate a conversation with other team members and explore how this may play out in teams. Often it emphasises how easily miscommunication can happen – especially without context.

# CHAPTER 4

# CONTEXT

In this chapter, we are going to look at:
- Ancient African wisdom captured with a word that has no direct English translation
- the surprising benefit of a questionable purpose
- treating your team like it's a rocket heading for space!

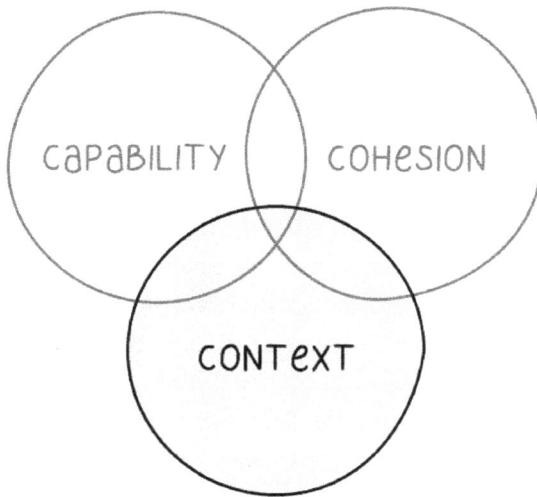

*Context is the hidden driver of team performance*

Melbourne has hosted the first Grand Prix of the Formula One season for most of the past 25 years. In March 2020, the stage was set for the opening round of the championship – an eagerly anticipated event where teams who have been working through the northern winter are keen to show the progress that they have made in the research and development of their cars. These are some of the most highly-tuned machines on the planet and having the best car on the grid with the best components is a huge advantage.

To make this even more explicit, in case you are not familiar with the sport, the same engine supplier (Ferrari, Mercedes, Honda or Renault) may supply multiple teams. That means that the difference in vehicle performance between cars with the same engine supplier relies heavily on what the team does to maximise the other components. As I'm sure you know, having a faster car that handles well and is reliable is a huge advantage in Formula One. The drivers' skills are important to success, but even I would beat Lewis Hamilton if we swapped his silver Mercedes F1 car for my silver Mazda.

OK, so it's clear that the engineering, design and manufacturing departments within Formula One teams are highly competitive with each other.

Within weeks of this scene, seven of these teams were in the United Kingdom back at their respective headquarters. Instead of competing, those teams had combined as a part of what was called 'Project Pitlane'[1], an industry-wide effort to manufacture and deliver respiratory devices to support the national need in response to the COVID-19 pandemic. These teams that were once intent on beating each other, and had spent millions of dollars trying to do so, had now joined forces.

What had changed? The context. Not just inside their team, but in their nation and on a global scale.

They remained highly skilled and capable engineers, designers and technicians with access to specialised equipment and resources. They possessed the ability to work together under pressure to build high performance components. What was required of them now was the ability to deploy their capability and cohesion in a new context.

# VALUE IS DELIVERED THROUGH CONTEXT

The benefits of team performance are realised because of – and in response to – context. Out of context, we can excel at irrelevant tasks. These Formula One teams could have kept working on their cars to make them faster for whenever the racing commenced. That would not have served the context that they found themselves in.

It is not only these world-class teams, there are stories across the globe of teams utilising their capability and cohesion to respond to the context of the global pandemic. Gin distilleries and beer breweries started producing hand sanitiser, community groups sewed personal protective equipment, restaurants made meals for healthcare workers despite being shut to customers. The list goes on and highlights the importance of being aware of and responsive to the context that our teams are in.

As we have discussed, the rate and magnitude of change we are experiencing is increasing. For this reason, the context that we are operating in is never stable and our teams need to be designed for a dynamic, adaptive way of working – not a fixed, linear or static approach.

# THE BEST TEAM IN THE WORLD

Here's a question for you to consider: Who is the best team in the world?

Which team did you nominate? Was it a sporting team, a business team, a medical team, a musical band or orchestra? Perhaps you thought of a scientific research team or an elite military squad. Whichever team you decided upon, it is almost impossible to have got that question right – or wrong! As we have already covered, teams exist in many settings across the world and being the best in the world depends significantly on what is required of the team.

For decades, the New Zealand All Blacks have been revered as a benchmark for sporting teams around the world and held up as an example of what teams could and should be like. That was only ever true in context: they have been the best *rugby* team. I wouldn't want that team operating on me or my family, in the same way that I wouldn't want a leading surgical team taking on international rugby teams. I also wouldn't want the New Zealand All Blacks team of 2020 to take on the New Zealand All Blacks of 2040. When the context shifts so significantly (from international rugby to surgery or over two decades), it is easy to appreciate that the context that a team operates in is important and influential.

**What is less obvious is that even with subtle changes in time, location and setting, the definition of world-class performance changes.**

In Seth Godin's short (but great) book, *The Dip,* he explores the idea of being the best in the world and why we all need to aim for that. Godin is principally a marketer (although his wisdom touches many other domains) and so this book talks about being the best in the world from a marketer's viewpoint. Very specifically, he talks about what he means by 'best' and perhaps more importantly what we mean by 'the world'. 'Best as in: best for them, right now, based on what they believe and what they know. The world as in: their world, the world they have access to.'[2]

It's not feasible for any individual or team to have the most impact in all circumstances, settings and situations. What we want is our teams to be the best in the world we inhabit, in the time and place that we find ourselves – in context.

## THE WORLD DON'T MOVE TO THE BEAT OF JUST ONE DRUM

Replicating what has led to success for others is very appealing – and the basis of many a marketing campaign. A simple trap to fall into is finding out what works in one team and trying to replicate it within our own. Unless the similarities are overwhelming, this sort of an approach is likely to fail. What is more useful is working to understand the principles behind a team's way of working in their environment and exploring how those principles may be applied in our teams.

On large scales, we have seen this play out. Australia voluntarily introduced cane toads into the environment. Given the ecologically disastrous impact that these animals have had across the continent, it may be hard to believe that they were brought in by choice. Of course, this impact wasn't the intended outcome. What was intended was that the toads would eat the cane beetles that were damaging sugar crops. That made some sense as toads do eat beetles. Turns out *these* toads don't eat *those* beetles and became a much bigger problem than the original beetles.

The point of this is to resist the urge of simply cutting and pasting solutions from other teams or other organisations. These duplicate solutions may work, but it's just as likely that there will be hidden and unexpected consequences of applying the same approach in a different setting. It comes back to applying principles, rather than assuming hard and fast rules about what will work for your teams.

## PAST PERFORMANCE IS NOT A RELIABLE INDICATOR OF FUTURE SUCCESS

The Australian Securities Investment Commission has specific guidance around how advertisers can use past performance within its material to indicate the suitability of a product for a consumer. This is particularly relevant for financial products and is why many of the advertisements contain wording along the lines of 'past performance is not a reliable indicator of future success'.

The advertisements don't mention this until after they've told us how much better off we would have been had we invested with them 10, 15 or 20 years ago – or how they have won awards in the past. They are obliged to tell us that their past performance is not a reliable indicator of future success and yet they use the exact opposite of that logic to convince us to invest in their products. The advertisers have made it clear what they think is going to be more likely to drive action – the appeal of doing what has worked in the past!

The same thing can happen in teams. Intellectually, we may know that our past success is no guarantee of future success, but behaviourally, we typically do the same things that led us to success in the past.

**Success can be a terrible teacher.
It rarely prompts us to reflect on
why we are getting the results, which
makes us very vulnerable to shifts
in context.**

There are many stories of companies that fell from grace because they hung onto outdated business models or product lines as they were seduced by past success – hello Kodak, Blockbuster and Nokia.

Of those three, only Nokia have made somewhat of a comeback, but they are a long way from their previous market-leading position. What these three companies have in common was a failure to respond to the shifting context in their market. It's easy to throw rocks from a distance and with the benefit of hindsight. The real trick for teams is to resist the comfort and complacency that can be brought on by success and constantly seek to deliver value in the current and emerging contexts that they are operating in.

# THE KEY ELEMENTS OF CONTEXT

We've looked at why context is so important for teams. Now, let's look at three elements that interact to create a team's context. These are:

- identity – who the team is both individually and collectively
- purpose – the reason that the team exists
- circumstances – factors within and beyond the team that impact on team performance.

## IDENTITY

Identity in teams is a two-way street. The strongest teams have a strong collective identity. They know who they are as a collective and have elements of their culture that are distinct and unique to that team (even within a larger organisation). Simultaneously, they allow individual members to feel they are accepted (dare we say celebrated?) for who they are and what they bring to their team. In later chapters, we will dive deeper into the value of leveraging true (not just surface) diversity.

For now, let's explore the idea of a team's identity. A strong sense of collective identity that reflects individual members is aligned directly to a number of aspects that make teams so useful including:

- shared accountability
- being greater than the sum of their parts
- innovation and creativity.

When we get it right, individuals need teams and teams need individuals.

### Uneven relationships are unstable

Most of us have a fairly strong sense of justice (and injustice). We like to have our efforts (physical, emotional, risk exposure) matched through an approximately equivalent reward. What this means for teams is that if team members are giving more of themselves than they are getting back in some form of reward, they are likely to adjust for this. For example they may:

- reduce the effort that they are putting into the work to match the reward they feel they are receiving
- find a new team to be a part of (quite possibly in a new organisation).

These are significant risks and opportunity costs in any team. But often they are either unseen or ignored.

The most powerful way that we can connect with team members is to have them feel that the team aligns with their own sense of who they are. When each team member sees that the team is a reflection of who they (and their team members) are, they are more committed and connected to the team.

We can equate this to other experiences in life such as being in a family, a religious group or a sporting club. We can see how we are a part of that group – and that group is a part of us. It's a rewarding and reaffirming experience that drives better effort and better results.

### Ubuntu

The concept of Ubuntu is an ancient philosophy that can be seen in various similar forms in southern, eastern, central and western African cultures. It is difficult to capture and directly translate to English, but its general principle can be summarised as the belief that 'a person is a person through other persons.' An even more concise way that it is often described is 'I am because we are'.

**The concept of Ubuntu has at its core that we are interconnected. Who I am is a reflection of the people that influence me. At the same time, those people are influenced by who I am.**

Despite its ancient roots, there is relevance to the Ubuntu approach in teams. This belief system is underpinned by the principles of humanism, complexity and systems thinking that are presented by academics and practitioners as being useful in a VUCA environment.

Promoting this intention within teams (that we are connected and that we are responsible for each other) is no mean feat and not for the faint-hearted. It takes courage and commitment from everyone – especially leaders. Specifically through the lens of identity, it elevates performance and commitment by seeing the work as more important than transactions. It allows that team to do work that no other team could do in that exact way – by virtue of the fact that the team accesses the unique elements of each person and that combination of people.

That's the whole point of high performing teams in any setting.

## PURPOSE

It seems self-evident that the reason a team exists influences the performance of a team. In fact, it is an essential component of the Katzenbach and Smith definition I cited in Chapter 1, that includes a team as being 'committed to a common purpose, performance goals and approach'. What is less obvious is that for high performance, not all purposes are created equal. High performing teams are best served by their purpose when they:

• own the purpose

- make it compelling
- make it questionable.

We will look briefly into these and how teams can apply and amplify the importance of purpose to drive performance.

### Own the purpose

Many teams are brought together by circumstances beyond their choosing. An organisation establishes a project or stream of work that they deem necessary. The members of the team are generally not self-selected (although the appointed leader is likely to have had a significant part in choosing who joins the team). What that means is that teams are often a group of people who have not chosen to work together, who are brought together to deliver something that they did not choose.

By itself, this is not a problem. It's the way of the world and doesn't prevent high performance. It's a starting point that great teams consider as something to build on.

A differentiator between average and great teams is that they take the initially inherited purpose and make it their own. They apply the inherited purpose and translate it into something that can guide goals, actions and ways of working. A purpose that is owned by the members of a team builds commitment (another essential component of teams). The way that many teams do this is by what Katzenbach and Smith call a 'purposing exercise' where the team is able to articulate what they want to achieve and why it means something to them.

It's important that this purpose is aligned to the members individually and collectively. It does not mean that the original intent of the inherited purpose is ignored or devalued. In fact, it is about lining up the purpose so that it adds value at individual, team and organisational levels.

*Make it compelling*

If you are seeking to learn more about teams, two researchers who are valuable to know about are Ruth Wageman and the late Richard Hackman. They have produced a number of research papers and books on team performance and team coaching. Much of their work is centred around why teams don't work and why they are not the solution to every problem.

These are important concepts to pay attention to. It's easy for many of us (myself included – perhaps especially people like me) to advocate that teams are the best solution for all problems. We have already discussed that some situations may better be suited to individual or group work.

In 2012, Richard Hackman produced a paper that presented the importance of six conditions (as opposed to causes) of team performance.[3] One of those six conditions was a compelling purpose. Not just any purpose – a compelling one. One that will guide the team to make the choices and take the actions that make a difference – even when it is difficult. This is entirely in line with what you would expect and what other researchers have found. It's also an indicator as to why so many teams that 'should' be high performing are not. Being a team is hard work and *if the reason to do that hard work doesn't connect with the team and its members, we can't expect exceptional performance* – even with the most talented and cohesive of teams.

*Make it questionable*

Ben Hunt-Davis has co-authored a book about his experience of winning gold at the Sydney 2000 Olympics with the Great Britain rowing team. The book is titled *Will it make the boat go faster?*[4] The title is a reflection of the question that guided the team throughout its whole preparation for the competition and towards its ultimate objective: to win a gold medal at the Sydney 2000 Olympics.

That purpose was clear. What was required to achieve that was for their boat to be the fastest on the water in that race. Therefore everything that they did in the lead up to that event was about making the boat go faster.

One of the many reasons that teams don't succeed is that members become individually busy, but not collectively productive. This story is a great example of how a clear and compelling purpose can guide teams to make choices and take actions that lead to the outcomes that they seek together. To be able to align their efforts with their objectives.

It's also a lesson in the power of questions. How effective would this have been as a statement? Something like 'make the boat go faster' doesn't sound as helpful in real time as that well-crafted question, 'will it make the boat go faster?'

**The right question allows every decision and every action to be put through the same test of ensuring that it aligns to the team's purpose.**

Spending time with your team to translate your compelling purpose into a powerful question is time and energy well spent.

## CIRCUMSTANCES

It would be easy to think of circumstances as a synonym for context. There is certainly overlap. The benefit of calling out circumstances is to help teams gain clarity by being more explicit about the forces influencing their performance. These forces can promote or hinder the ability of any team to achieve its objectives.

In broad terms, we can consider the circumstances that teams face along two axes. Firstly, are the influencing circumstances internal or external – are they coming from within the team or from beyond the team? Secondly, are those influences having a positive or negative impact on the team's performance.

While it's more convenient to consider circumstances as independent to other elements of the team's context – identity and purpose – the fact is that these all interact with each other and are responsive to each other. If we consider this in even a little more detail, it becomes clear.

- A team's purpose is inherently influenced by its circumstances.
- Those circumstances include the identity of the team and its members.

It's possible to go even deeper, but the point among this complexity is a relatively simple one – the circumstances of the team are important to performance. Those circumstances have an influence on other elements of a team's context.

### Messy is a feature, not a bug

The context of a team is not a balanced composition of identity, purpose and circumstances. It's a messy interaction of those three elements. In modern teams, it is common for lines of responsibility to be blurred or unclear. This is a challenge to operate in. But here's a tip.

## The best teams do more than accept the mess, they embrace it.

They consider the messiness a feature, not a bug. Think of it as printing in colour. If we are limited only to red, green and blue, the quality of the images that we can produce is restricted. When we use different mixtures of these same colours, we can create thousands of different colours that can be used in more ways.

This metaphor is apt for our teams. The components are important. The combination and interaction of those components is how we can become greater than the sum of our parts.

It is useful to keep this concept of messy interaction in mind when we consider the circumstances of any team.

It's self-evident that a team is influenced by its members. What isn't always as obvious (despite being simultaneously true) is that the members of the team are influenced by the team. If we look a bit closer, we can see that the team as a whole is also influenced by individual connections between members. If we zoom out a bit further, we can see that the team is influenced by the wider environment in which it operates, such as the organisation, and that the organisation is influenced by things beyond it, such as competitors, governments and technology.

The temptation to consider these as linear connections is strong and appealing. It's nice to think of each of these as links in a chain that connect sequentially on either side...

- individuals interact with their team
- teams interact with other teams in the same organisation
- the organisation has a consistent and centralises interaction with the external environment.

But as we think this through, it's clear this is not the case. Each layer interacts with all of the others. There is no doubt that individuals are affected by the external environment (such as shifts in technological, social and political factors) and the organisations that they work in – and vice versa. It's useful to keep in mind that a team's circumstances are the whole (not just the parts) of what is happening both inside the team (individual and team levels) as well as outside (immediate and wider environments).

### Fuel and friction

Dan Ariely of Duke University and author of *Predictably Irrational* (plus several other books) presented a TED Talk in 2019[5] on behaviour change that presents a useful way for teams to look at performance. Ariely talks about fuel being things that help behaviour change (and hence we want to maximise) and friction slowing behaviour change (and hence try to minimise). Here's how it's useful for understanding your team's circumstances.

If we consider the team's purpose as equivalent to behaviour change, there will be a number of factors (circumstances) that are providing 'fuel' – as in driving the team towards its objectives. These might be external factors, such as rewards from the organisation, or internal, such as the capabilities within the teams. Likewise, there will be forces that slow the team down that could come from beyond the team, such as changes to government regulation, or within the team such as poor information sharing or collaboration.

The exercise at the end of this chapter is a great way to map these forces. Once they are mapped, it's possible to better make a decision about the best actions for a team at any given time. It's important to regularly revisit these circumstances. The world changes fast and there is a huge risk that without being attentive to the shifting circumstances around a team, we become elite at solving yesterday's problems.

# EMPOWERED THROUGH CONTEXT

*Team of Teams* is a book that tells the story of the American Joint Forces in Iraq from 2004 onwards.[6] In a nutshell, it describes how the best resourced military force ever known to humans was being defeated by untrained militia with bad guns. It's now my second favourite book on teams (you're reading my new favourite!). One of the many lessons is that the US military forces needed to adapt the way that they operated in response to the context in which they found themselves.

No longer was it enough for forces on the ground to simply execute on the order that they had been given. By the time directives had reached troops, the information was obsolete and the target had moved on. What was required was a dramatically different way of working that challenged a lot of the beliefs and practices that had served military teams so well for so long. It became insufficient for troops to simply obey orders. They learned this lesson: teams can be efficient, but ineffective.

What was required was for troops to make decisions and take actions that were in the best interest of the mission. This was a shift that required empowering people closer to the action. As it is beautifully stated in the book, 'people can only be effectively empowered if they have enough context to make good decisions'.

This need for empowerment through context saw the commanding officers dramatically shift the way that they shared information (both inside and outside of their organisation). The responsibility that they gave to teams on the ground was unprecedented – and uncomfortable. For an organisation built on hierarchy, this was a very big shift away from what they had known and what had been successful for so long.

## Increased visibility of context throughout the teams allowed what was termed 'empowered execution'.

This approach allowed the teams to operate in a more responsive way and without needing to engage senior leaders for routine (and often not very routine) decision making. In turn, this freed up leaders to concentrate more on the strategic direction and creating the conditions that allowed more of the teams to operate with visibility of the context. It was an upward spiral.

Another benefit was that with an increased visibility of the broader context, teams that previously coveted information and resources were willing and able to share these for the greater good of the mission. With the same level of resources, more was getting done.

## RECAP

# CONTEXT IS TOO IMPORTANT TO IGNORE

Context is the hidden driver of performance for great teams. While it's not always obvious from the outside, and may feel less tangible than other elements of performance like the capability or cohesion of the team, context is too important to ignore. Without having clarity around a team's identity, purpose and circumstances it is possible to be very efficient at executing on tasks that lack relevance. We can be solving yesterday's challenges instead of today's and tomorrow's. That is a recipe for irrelevance.

Committing energy, attention and time to being responsive to the context of your teams is an investment in its effectiveness. It unlocks many of the benefits of teams – such as focusing on outcomes not processes, building resilience through better use of information and resources and improved collective intelligence. There is far more to operating as a team than context, but without context, our teams are unable to deliver on their potential.

## REVIEW QUESTIONS

Use these questions to capture your own thoughts or facilitate a conversation with your team.

### IDENTITY

- How can you elevate the humanity in your team?
- What would you love (and hate) about being your own teammate?
- Does your team make each individual better (and vice versa)?

### PURPOSE

- Does your team own its purpose?
- Is your team's purpose compelling?
- Can you use your team's purpose to guide actions and decisions in real time?

### CIRCUMSTANCES

- What are the forces that are driving this team towards its objectives?
- Are there any things making it hard to succeed in this team?
- Are you paying enough attention to both the people and the environment in your team's performance?

## ACTIVITY – FUEL AND FRICTION

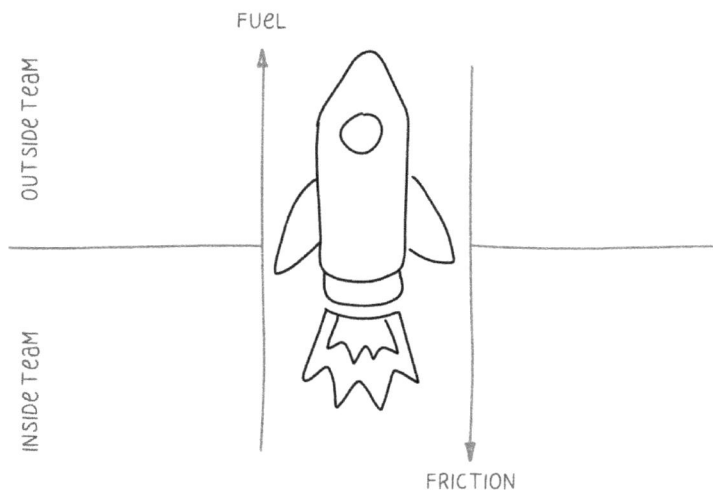

FUeL

OUTSIDe TeaM

INSIDe TeaM

FRICTION

### PURPOSE

Use this activity as a way of:

- exploring what is helping the team
- having an explicit conversation about the things that are slowing the team down
- considering actions to either increase fuel or reduce friction within the team.

### WHAT YOU'LL NEED

- flip chart or whiteboard
- pens/markers for participants
- 5+ people
- 15 – 30 minutes

## INSTRUCTIONS

### STEP 1

Ask participants to individually reflect on what things are helping the team achieve its objectives. Participants should consider factors that are both:

- internal to the team
- external to the team.

### STEP 2

Ask participants to individually reflect on what things are making it difficult for the team to achieve its objectives. Participants should consider factors that are both:

- internal to the team
- external to the team.

### STEP 3

Get participants to place their sticky notes on the flip chart / board in the corresponding areas.

As they place them, ask participants to group similar answers together.

Identify (or get a participant to identify) 2–3 themes for each question.

### STEP 4

Facilitate a discussion about implications of this for this team / organisation.

Develop an action plan.

# CHAPTER 5

# COHESION

In this chapter, we are going to look at:
- why failing well is crucial to team performance
- how too much cohesion can hurt teams
- the paradox of structure.

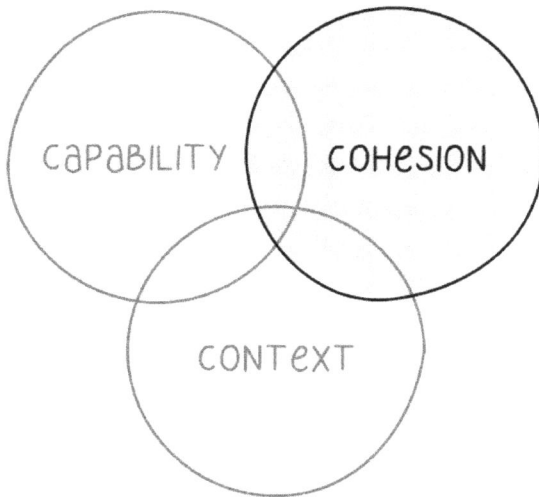

*Teams can be greater than the sum of their parts, but not by accident.*

I love trivia.

By that I mean that I love both random bits of information as well as trivia quizzes. For a while, I have had a theory about the ultimate trivia team. I reckon that, ideally, there are a bunch of people who:

- are known to each other but not necessarily close friends (probably connected through mutual friends)
- love trivia independently
- each knows a lot about certain (different) things
- each knows what the other members' specialty topics are. Here's what I imagine happens in that scenario:
- people like each other, but come for the trivia as well as the company
- collectively, the team knows far more than they do individually
- they don't argue over what the capital of Kazakhstan is because they trust that Joanne is their geography person.

Here's how it might differ from a team that is made up of people with similar interests, similar backgrounds and with strong friendships. These teams tend to:

- come to catch up with each other (the trivia is an added bonus)
- have deep knowledge in the same topic areas
- have shallow or very limited knowledge in other areas
- develop patterns where the dominant personalities (or those who put together better arguments) tend to have the casting vote.

I think that you know where I am heading here. Diversity of thought, background and world views is important to pub trivia teams as well as your teams in business. It's not just the diversity, it's also creating the environment where that diversity can be utilised and applied. It makes you more ready to answer more questions. In trivia, you only need one person to know each answer – you don't get bonus points if everyone knows David Bowie's neighbour's name!

In Australia, our politicians are fond of 'the pub test', which is supposed to test how the public would really respond to an issue. Not sure how well that works, but I think that there might be some merit in teams considering a 'pub trivia test'.

# GREATER THAN THE SUM OF THEIR PARTS

This idea of the pub trivia test is a good one to keep in mind. It highlights the importance of not only having a group of people or even the right mix of people, but also creating the conditions for a group of people to deliver great collective outcomes. One of the defining characteristics of teams is that they are able to be better together than they are apart. In other words, they need to be cohesive.

An easy assumption to make is that bringing together hard working, smart and talented people will guarantee high levels of performance. It can and does happen, but it's not guaranteed.

One of the earliest and most repeated studies in social psychology looked into the concept of *social loafing*. The idea is that when people are part of a group, they are inclined to exert less effort than if they are working independently. Repeated studies over more than a century have shown this phenomenon to hold up across a range of activities including pulling ropes, clapping and even shouting! Consistently, we can see people putting in less effort and the group being significantly less than the sum of its parts.

A related concept is *social facilitation* – the idea that an individual increases their effort and performance in the presence of others. This has also been studied and replicated consistently for a long time. With diverse activities such as cycling and word association, it has been demonstrated that the presence of others has been a useful factor in performance. I experience this with tasks like running or going to the gym – I'm far more likely to do it and do it better with someone else compared to going solo. You can probably think of some examples when this happens for you.

Social facilitation is about the presence of others, but not necessarily working with them. Does that mean that we do tasks better independently with others in the vicinity? Sometimes, but there is more to it.

Recent research supports the fact that – in the right conditions – teams are collectively more intelligent, more productive and more profitable than individuals or less cohesive groups. As Sandy Pentland from MIT's Human Dynamics Laboratory points out in *Harvard Business Review*, 'individual reasoning and talent contribute far less to team success than one might expect.'[1]

It's possible to dive into this rabbit hole much deeper, but all that we need to know is that both social loafing and social facilitation exist.[2] We don't need to explore exactly why that might be the case at this stage. It's also necessary for us to appreciate that it has been demonstrated that we are capable of being greater than the sum of our parts.

It's a case of when, not if. In our teams, we need to be cognisant of *when* our teams are greater than the sum of their parts. What are the conditions that support this? How can we make it happen more often and tap into the benefits of working as a team – for individuals and organisations? How can we avoid the traps of social loafing (and other phenomena) that have the potential to make bringing people together an unrewarding experience for all involved?

## MEANINGFUL DIVERSITY

Diverse teams perform better than less diverse teams. They also perform worse. That seems like a contradiction, but what I mean is this:

## Diversity alone is not sufficient to experience improved performance.

Having a team with a mix of ages, cultures, genders, sexuality or professions does not guarantee success. The benefits of diversity rely on many factors, including members taking approaches that allow diverse perspectives to be used within the team.

The pub trivia team doesn't get better just because there are members who know more answers. We need those members to be able to share what they know. Just as importantly, we need those members to be heard and for their perspectives to be taken on board. Then, we can win the drinks voucher. In our work teams, tapping into diverse perspectives means that we can achieve more together than we could apart.

## EFFECTIVE PARTNERING

Global advisory firm Gartner released some compelling research in 2020 that highlights that simply throwing diverse teams together is insufficient. Their global survey on leader effectiveness, which surveyed 2819 leaders, revealed a number of valuable findings that highlight the importance of cohesion – and the need for deliberate approach to achieve it.[3]

They explored an approach to leadership that they referred to as complementary leadership, which they defined as 'the intentional partnership between one leader and one or many leader partners to share leadership responsibilities based on complementary skill sets.'

It's as though they have taken a thesaurus to the Katzenbach and Smith definition I cited in Chapter 1. They're talking about leadership teams, not leadership groups. Here are a few key points from their research:

- 48% of the impact a leader has on team performance can be attributed to sharing responsibilities with others who have complementary skills sets.
- Almost three-quarters of leaders are either not partnering at all or partnering ineffectively.
- 29% of leaders exercise complementary leadership effectively, boosting their team performance to 13% above average.

The upshot of all of this is pretty compelling. Effective performance relies on leaders taking a team approach.

## Crucially, it is not enough to just partner – partnering ineffectively actually led to below average performance.

While this is specifically in relation to leadership teams, this point is pertinent. If leadership teams are not modelling effective partnering, then it is less likely that other teams in the organisation are being encouraged and supported to operate as truly interdependent teams.

# CREATING COHESION – THREE KEY ELEMENTS

So far, we have discussed the importance of cohesion to team performance. Let's look at what we can do to create the conditions for cohesion in our teams. These are the three key elements that we will explore:

- psychological safety – raising the cost of silence
- connections – creating pathways for cooperation and collaboration within, between and beyond teams
- structures – the routines, rhythms and rituals that enable a cohesive and flexible way of working together.

# PSYCHOLOGICAL SAFETY

Psychological safety has got a lot of attention in the world of leadership and team performance in recent years. Most of that can be traced back to Google's work in Project Aristotle[4] where they set about finding out what made their teams effective. The number one factor that they identified was psychological safety. Psychological safety has turned up consistent and robust results in many team settings (healthcare, education, military, business) and seems to be gaining momentum in both academic and business circles.

Like many concepts that become popular, psychological safety has experienced a bit of hype around it, it has been interpreted in various ways and it has been around much longer than the 2016 release of the Google findings. For these reasons, it is valuable to get clear on what psychological safety is (and isn't), what it offers teams and some ways that you can foster it within your teams.

In other words, let's get clear on:

- *what* psychological safety is
- *why* it matters for your teams
- *how* to take actions and increase the likelihood of safety in your teams.

## WHAT – DEFINING PSYCHOLOGICAL SAFETY

Psychological safety has the air of 'fluffy stuff' about it. It gives some people the impression that it is all about being nice to each other and not about real work. It's neither of these things and it is worth exploring that a little further.

Professor Amy Edmondson of Harvard Business School is the most prominent researcher in the field of psychological safety. It is not a concept that she came up with, but it is one that she has spent more than two decades researching and writing about. For that reason, I sought out her work to get clear on how to define this idea so that teams can operate more effectively. In a 2014 review titled 'Psychological Safety: The History, Renaissance, and Future of an Interpersonal Construct'[5] Edmondson and her colleague Zhike Lei define psychological safety as: 'People's perceptions of the consequences of taking interpersonal risks in a particular context'.

In other words, 'Am I OK to take risks here?' That is, do I feel safe at a personal level? In a team setting, Edmondson's canonic 1999 paper on the topic defines it in a similar, but different, way: 'A shared belief held by members of a team that the team is safe for interpersonal risk taking.'[6] The difference is that it's a *shared belief* that everyone is safe. So the question shifts from, 'Am I OK...' to 'Are we OK to take risks here?'

A useful way to think about psychological safety in teams is as 'raising the cost of silence'. In other words, it becomes more expensive for team members to remain silent and less expensive for team members to speak up. This is a great test for your own team. Do members feel that they can raise concerns, questions and mistakes freely? Or do they feel it is better to resolve or cover up their concerns, questions and mistakes without raising them?

By looking at the many stories of corporate whistleblowers – and how many of those end up paying a huge financial and psychological price for speaking up – it's possible to realise that in many environments, people are not OK to share openly and take risks. In these environments, there is no safety. Thinking about psychological safety this way gives more toughness to the concept. It's often more difficult and takes more courage to say something – especially when that exposes team members in some way. In a psychologically safe environment, members speak up if they think their leader has made a mistake, if they have made a mistake, if they have an idea that might help, or if they have noticed that something is wrong.

## WHY – LINKING SAFETY AND PERFORMANCE

When members are able to speak up and take risks, many positive outcomes are associated with it. As already noted, it was a key finding of Google's Project Aristotle and aligns to the findings of Atlassian (the multi-billion dollar software company that develop products for teams) who describe the benefits of working 'open' – impossible without psychological safety.

### Safety leads to performance

Numerous studies have correlated psychological safety with performance in teams. Among others, there are findings that link safety to learning, innovation, cooperation, information sharing and trust. This is not an exhaustive list, but you can see from these alone that many of the benefits of teams and why they matter can

rates. How could that be? It goes against a lot of what we might expect. Surely the better teams make fewer mistakes? Until we dig a little bit deeper. It's important to remember that those were the teams that *reported* the highest error rate. This is likely to be different to the actual error rate. If we can assume that error rates are similar across teams (with similarly experienced and skilled professionals), then the reported error rate is more reflective of the response that the team and its members have to failure. The problem is not errors (everyone is likely to make them), the problem is in sharing them.

## Teams can't learn from what doesn't get shared.

The best teams spend less time covering up or pretending that mistakes haven't happened. They spend more time acknowledging them, sharing them, learning from them and adapting to improve their performance (i.e. learning!).

# CONNECTIONS

In 2015, I was part of a team called Shinobi at the company that I worked at (you can check me out on LinkedIn if you really want to know the company). We were a part of an internal program of nine self-nominated teams that set about shifting the internal performance of the company. As part of that program, all teams were challenged with embarking on a project that would make a commercial difference (either increase revenue or decrease costs). While other teams came up with some great ideas that were directly related to the bottom line in the short term (like reducing the spend on taxis from airports to offices), Shinobi concluded that the best thing that we could do was to *Create Better Connections*.

We found that poor connections and poor coordination were costing us millions of dollars. There were instances where procurement was slow or where we didn't use our combined buying power to negotiate a better deal with suppliers. On other occasions, we didn't know that customers used multiple products of ours – because different teams were responsible for different products and didn't have a connection – so customers wouldn't get the best service from either. We discovered that different parts of the organisation were making similar errors because there was no way for that information to be shared.

While it isn't as tangible as saving money on taxis, connections are a significant opportunity in most organisations. The same principle applies at team level.

## THE IMPACT OF HUMAN DYNAMICS

In the *Harvard Business Review* article that I referenced earlier in this chapter, Sandy Pentland of MIT dives into his team's study of the communication patterns that are 'observable, quantifiable, and measurable' in high performing teams. There are specific patterns of interaction that indicate a high performing team. In other words, if you want a better team, create better connections. Team Shinobi were definitely onto something!

Keeping the idea of better connections in mind is useful. Diving another layer deeper allows us to be more specific and takes this from a concept into concrete actions. Specifically, Pentland and his team found that the best teams displayed three patterns – energy, engagement and exploration.

## LEVELS OF DYNAMICS

On top of considering these levels of dynamics as energy, engagement and exploration it is worth also considering them in relation to the team boundaries. These levels of dynamics translate almost (but not entirely) perfectly to creating connections within teams, between teams and beyond the organisation. In other words, create better connections:

- *Within* your team by focusing on the energy that team members share with each other – how and how often they interact.
- *Between* teams within your organisation by supporting engagement. This requires engagement in both directions – to the team and its purpose, as well as to teams that you need to partner with like other departments within your organisation.
- *Beyond* your team and organisation by encouraging exploration. This allows teams to interact beyond the organisation's boundaries and bring diverse perspectives into decisions and actions.

I have taken a little bit of poetic licence here, but I am confident that this is a useful way to look at your team's connections. The diagram below is a summary of this and is a good reminder that it's important to start within the team itself. The strength of connections radiates out from the team's energy. Commit to this, support this and the benefits of strong team connections at all levels are amplified.

## TOO MUCH OF A GOOD THING

While the focus on internal connections within a team is important, and the foundation of great connections beyond the team, it also comes with a risk attached. It is possible (and common) for teams to become too well connected with each other. It's the classic Goldilocks metaphor. Too little connection within the team and

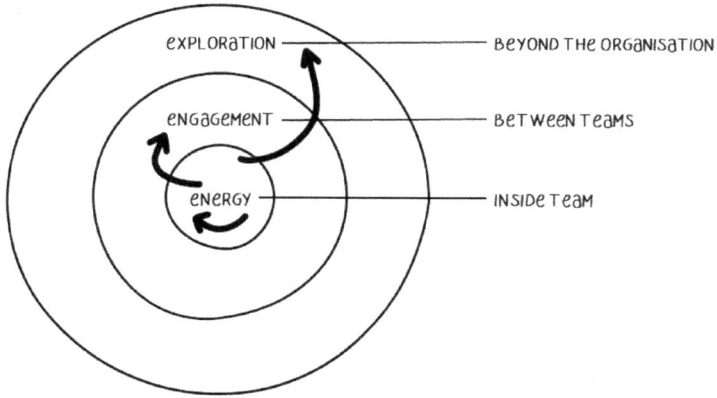

*The strength of connections radiates out from a team's energy.*

performance suffers because members aren't able to work well together. Too much connection and teams can develop tunnel vision. They can become too defensive of their own team's approach and lose the benefits of external perspectives.

A great and succinct way that this is summarised in the book *Team of Teams* is when they describe world-class military teams – Army Rangers, Navy SEALs and so on – who don't collaborate well. It was actually a by-product of strong connections within each of the teams. As one Navy SEAL put it... 'the squad is at the point which everyone else sucks. That other squadron sucks, the other SEAL team sucks, and our Army counterparts definitely suck.'

If this is the experience within your teams, beware. Without a deliberate approach you can easily create an echo chamber where you tell each other that you are great and doing great things while everyone else is hopeless. The danger is that this feeling is seductive. It's a feeling we are drawn to. In an interconnected world, it's a recipe for ineffectiveness.

## SIZE MATTERS

There is plenty to suggest that the size of a team matters – for various tasks there are various optimal numbers. My advice on this is to let that be guided by the team's context and have one more team member than would make the team ineffective. Go as lean as possible. Be very wary of falling into the trap that more people are going to get the job done better or quicker. Just like too many cooks can spoil a broth, too many team members can slow decisions and unnecessarily complicate coordinating actions.

One of the reasons that larger teams can lose effectiveness can be seen by considering Metcalfe's Law. This is a formula that has been used to calculate the number of potential connections within a communication network. The numbers work for teams also. For the mathematically inclined, here is the formula:

*Possible connections = n(n-1)/2*
*(where n = the number of team members)*
For the rest of us, here's what that means.

## The number of possible connections within teams increases exponentially as members increase.

For example:
- 2 team members = 1 connection
- 3 team members = 2 connections
- 5 team members = 10 connections
- 10 team members = 45 connections
- 20 team members = 190 connections

As we have just explored, connections between team members are central to high performing teams. The more connections, the less likely that members are able to commit time and attention to them and hence they are not likely to be strong. To tap into the benefits of team performance, keep your connections to the optimal level for your context – and no more.

# STRUCTURES

Within cohesion, we have looked at the role of safety and connections in allowing teams to work better together. The final component of cohesion for us to consider is structures. What I am talking about here is not the structure on an organisational chart. I am talking about the frameworks that teams operate within in order to get work done.

While I personally resist structure – I prefer to be far more ad hoc and 'go with the flow' – I have observed and come to learn the value of structure. I wish that it wasn't true, but structure allows us to do more work and better work – both individually and collectively.

## Ironically and paradoxically, structure gives us freedom.

The right structures give clarity on what we need to do, when we need to do it and how we need to do it. Let's explore three levels of structures that help teams perform at their best together:
- routines – what the team does
- rhythms – how often those actions happen
- rituals – what the team recognises and rewards.

The combination of these structures reduces the cognitive load and increases confidence for each team member.

## ROUTINES GIVE US PLACE

Routines are the actions that a team takes regularly. Typically, they may include things like team meetings, project reviews, one-to-one meetings between the leader and each member. The purpose that they serve is to orient (or re-orient) us in terms of the work that we are doing. It's a bit like the recap at the start of a TV series that says, 'Previously on *The Good Place...*' We look back and see where we have been and what we have done. More importantly, we discuss what we need to do from here. Once we are clearer on our sense of place, we are able to move forward with confidence and this is the important function of strong routines.

## RHYTHMS SET THE PACE

While routines are what teams do, rhythms are how often those actions take place. Together, they set a team's schedule. For example, the routine is a team meeting, the rhythm for that may be weekly. As a result, weekly team meetings become part of the schedule.

One dictionary definition for rhythm includes that it is '...a strong, regular, repeated pattern'. For teams, this is a powerful idea. What needs to become a strong, regular and repeated pattern? One beat of one drum is not very effective. The repeated beating of a drum in a pattern becomes something we can dance to. A dozen drums beating to the same pattern becomes hypnotic and inspirational.

## RITUALS SEND SIGNALS

Routines, rhythms and now onto rituals. Rituals are events that take place in order to recognise or acknowledge certain events. In any group, the rituals that we have and what we choose to celebrate in some way send signals about what we value and what is important. We can think about in many domains of life:

- Families celebrate Mother's Day together because they want to show their mum that she is valued and appreciated.
- Religions have annual pilgrimages, holidays or traditions.
- Countries have public holidays to commemorate events such as independence or the end to a war.
- Sporting clubs sing victory songs that connect them to the origins of the club.

In a team setting, our rituals send stronger signals than the words we use about what is important and valued. If a leader says, 'We are innovative and take appropriate risks,' and yet only celebrates and acknowledges successful projects, it is a missed opportunity. We want to be able to celebrate and reward success. In the 2020s, we also need to acknowledge and celebrate the right risks, efforts and even failure. My favourite example of a ritual that sends a signal about the value of effort and failure is a 'Failure Wall' that Jeff Stibel started at Dun & Bradstreet.[8] The idea was to demonstrate that failure is an important, valued and normal part of operating. It helped others to share and learn from their mistakes and reduce the desire to play small more readily.

This is the difference that well selected rituals can make. Actions send signals about what is important, that put words into practice. The rituals of your team are worth considering. Celebrating success is highly recommended. Please do it – often and wholeheartedly. Appropriately supporting an environment where failure is considered a valuable part of learning is equally important and far less common.

Please don't let this example limit your imagination on the rituals that will serve your teams. Think of what is important to you and consider ways to put that into action so you can send strong and consistent messages that guide team members to the right way of working.

## RECAP

# COHESION IS BOTH AN INPUT AND OUTPUT OF HIGH PERFORMING TEAMS

Through psychological safety, connections and structures, teams achieve a superior way of working in comparison to more traditional centralised models.

- Psychological safety leads to benefits including trust, learning and innovation.
- Connections lead to better information sharing, decision making and shared accountability.
- Structures free teams up to do their best work together.

The inverse is also true in that the high performance of teams (not just the results, but how they get them) are inherently cohesive. It's not possible to be greater than the sum of our parts without cohesion. Experiencing the benefits of cohesion reinforces the benefits of this way of working and makes teams more likely to increase safety, connections and use structures.

We have seen in this chapter that diversity and partnering alone are not enough. Ineffective partnering can be worse for some teams than working independently. The time, effort and energy required for working together needs to deliver a return or it is a waste. If teams are not prepared to commit to the actions that drive cohesion, they may be better off working independently.

# REVIEW QUESTIONS

Use these questions to capture your own thoughts or facilitate a conversation with your team.

## PSYCHOLOGICAL SAFETY

- Is it OK to take risks in your teams?
- What impact would maintaining or improving a high level of psychological safety make to your teams?
- How can you raise the cost of silence in your teams?

## CONNECTIONS

On a scale from 0 (strongly disagree) to 10 (strongly agree) what is your response to the following statements?

- Your teams have strong connections between all members.
- Your teams have strong connections within your organisation.
- Your teams have strong connections beyond your organisation.

## STRUCTURES

On a scale from 0 (strongly disagree) to 10 (strongly agree) what is your response to the following statements?

- Your teams have strong routines that provide a sense of place.
- Your teams have strong rhythms that provide the right pace of work.
- Your teams have strong rituals that send signals aligned to your values.

## BONUS QUESTION

Would your team win a pub trivia quiz? Extra bonus points if you find out!

## ACTIVITY – DRAW YOUR TEAM

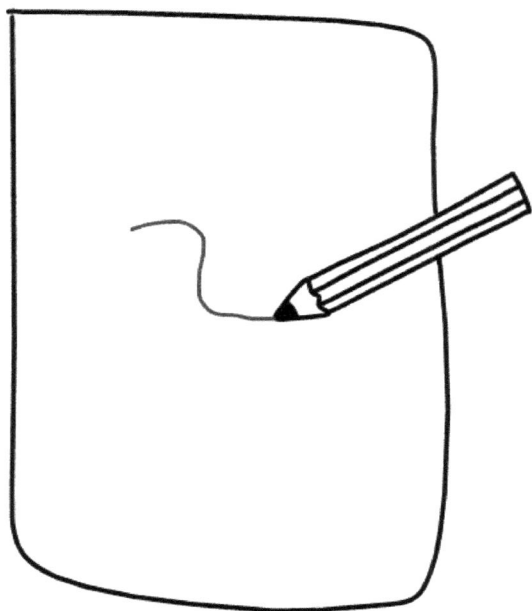

### PURPOSE

Use this activity as a way of:

- allowing each member to reflect on the team and how the team is currently working together
- identifying similar and divergent perceptions of how the team is operating
- facilitating a discussion to develop an action plan for how the team can operate in a more cohesive way.

## WHAT YOU'LL NEED

- A3 or A4 paper (one per participant)
- pens/markers for participants (multiple colours for each participant)
- 5+ people
- 15 – 30 minutes

## INSTRUCTIONS

### STEP 1

Ask participants to individually reflect on the team and how the team is currently working together.

### STEP 2

Have participants draw an image that represents how they observe that the team is operating.

Participants should consider factors including:

- their personal experience in the team
- observations of members of the team – and how they interact
- how the team is engaging with stakeholders external to the team.

Note: The image does not need to be literal and it may be useful for participants to consider:

- use of metaphors (tools, vehicles, animals)
- the colours and shapes that they use to convey meaning
- avoid using names (including their own) and words.

**STEP 3**

Present the images for participants to be able to see all images.

Note: Depending on the space you are working with, a wall or table works well or you may consider presenting them around the room as a pop-up gallery.

**STEP 4**

Ask participants to view all of the images silently and reflect on what they notice. Some useful prompts include:

- Are there any common themes?
- Are there conflicting themes?
- Are they surprised by anything?
- What questions do they have for the team?

**STEP 5**

Facilitate a group discussion about implications of this for this team.

Develop an action plan.

# CHAPTER 6

# CAPABILITY

In this chapter, we are going to look at:
- why capability is about more than just the skills that team members bring
- how Austin Powers can teach our teams a lesson on managing capacity
- why playing to strengths can be both a good and bad idea for your teams.

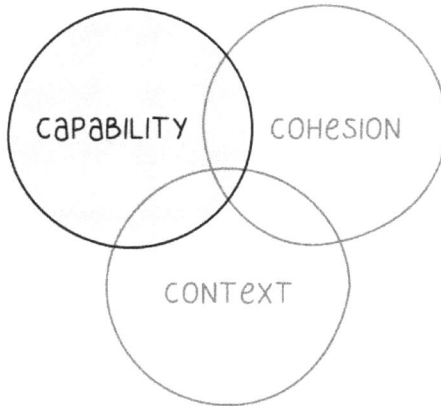

*Capability in our teams needs to be constantly dynamic and developing.*

Canadian circus company, Cirque du Soleil are the poster child of 'Blue Ocean Strategy' – creating a new and different market that they have gone on to dominate. A major point of difference between Cirque du Soleil and traditional circuses (circii?) is that there are no animals. It is an upmarket performance and a celebration of amazing human feats.

To achieve that, Cirque du Soleil needs to recruit the best of the best. According to their website, in 2020, across their various shows, the company's 1300 performers come from 55 countries. They span disciplines including sport, circus arts, dance and music.

These people are often world-class performers in their own rights – for example, the cast includes Olympic gold medalists. The equivalent applies for circus performers, dancers, musicians, clowns, actors and other talents. Each of the shows has a cast of 50 to 100 performers who come together to create incredible experiences.

As you read this, you will realise that in the context of Cirque du Soleil, *being a world class performer is taken for granted*. If you are not in the elite of your particular field, you are not even getting invited to the auditions. To actually get into that team (the cast), you need to be the best of those people. That gets you a place on the stage – literally.

It's not enough, though. Those skills need to be developed. You will need to learn to coordinate and deliver with a group of other performers that you have not previously worked with, creating new shows that have never even existed before. These are new skills.

This is not unique to circus performers. The same applies to medical professionals learning new techniques or how to administer new drugs. The same applies to software developers having to learn new platforms and create programs for new operating systems. Likewise, a legal team taking on a new case or responding to new legislation, or a construction team learning how to build with new equipment. Across industries and settings, teams need a base level of skill if they are going to achieve results.

# SKILLS – BUT NOT JUST SKILLS

When I talk about a team's capability, I am referring to the ability of team members to perform relevant tasks for the team's objectives.

What we can see from the circus story is that the ability to perform the right tasks for the team and with the team is essential for high performance. It seems fairly obvious that the ability for team members to do the job that the team requires sits at the heart of it. The fact that capability is visible means that it's often the first place that people look to develop their teams. What we will see is that there are some nuances to the role of capability in teams and how to develop it. If you are able to appreciate and respond to the more complex role of capability, your teams will be able to perform better now and also as the demands on the teams change.

Here are some of the subtleties that we will dig into:

### Capability is connected to context and cohesion

Which skills do your team need? It depends on what you are trying to achieve, of course. The actual capabilities that teams are required to possess and develop are directly connected to the context of the team. It's no good if an orchestra has the world's best mechanics. Likewise, the ability of those team members to operate together is what makes that team greater than the sum of its parts. It's also no good if the orchestra are playing different pieces of music at different rhythms.

*Capability is more than just the skills of individual team members*
When we think about the team's capability, we need to consider how well those team members can be coordinated to work together. We also need to look beyond just the skills. The ability to perform is also a function of the team's capacity (any overworked team will drop in performance) and the ability to leverage strengths.

*Developing capability is a meta-skill of teaming*
The ability for a team to continue to develop its capability is increasingly important. This is connected to the fact that capability is inherently connected to context. If a team's context is never static, it makes sense that the capabilities required to perform in that context are also never static.

## THREE TYPES OF SKILLS

As part of an advisory for human resources executives for 2019,[1] Gartner described three types of skills that organisations need to be aware of. The categories are useful at a team level also. They are:

- evolving
- emerging
- expiring.

Let's look briefly into these. I'll give a few examples, but I'm not assuming that these are relevant for your team. Once again, the context is all important. The three questions on skills at the end of this chapter form a great exercise to consider what these might be for your team. You can do it alone, individually with team members or as a whole team – depending on the context, of course!

### Evolving skills

These are the skills that have been serving teams and team members well that will need to remain relevant in the foreseeable future. This might be something like a marketing team that needs to continue to learn how to produce content for social media channels.

### Emerging skills

These are the skills that are on the horizon for a team and its members as things change. That same marketing team may need to understand new social media channels or the use of artificial intelligence to better communicate with their target market.

### Expiring skills

These are the skills that have become irrelevant (or are rapidly becoming so). For the marketing team, it might be the ability to design and deliver campaigns for traditional media such as print newspapers.

As an aside, apparently Chief Marketing Officers (CMOs) have the shortest average tenure of all C-Level executives according to a 2017 Forbes article that cites a Korn Ferry report. The main reason? Staying relevant. According to the article, 'CMOs who stick with yesterday's strategies deserve distrust and are themselves likely to be gone in a few years.'[2]

All of this underscores that skills are never stagnant. We need to pay close attention to all three categories and ensure that our efforts are appropriately matched. There is no point investing in expiring skills or ignoring emerging skills if we want to maintain our team's relevance and effectiveness.

## LEARNING AND UNLEARNING

What becomes apparent as we look at skills through the lenses of evolving, emerging and expiring is that skill acquisition is central for team performance. We need to be able to learn (and unlearn) at a rate that matches the demands on the team.

### Learning

Learning is essential for team performance and it is an output of high performing teams. Unfortunately, learning also has a brand problem. Too many people think of learning as sitting down in a classroom and having knowledge imparted upon them. That's another legacy of the industrial revolution, when schooling became about ensuring that enough of the population was able to take instructions to operate in the factories and on the production lines. The assumption being that the person leading the lesson has all of the answers and that those answers will also remain constant.

In the 2020s, neither of those assumptions is safe. The rate of change in the world (political, technological and social) mean that information becomes irrelevant faster than ever. What is more relevant is to define learning as *progress towards mastery*. The ability to complete tasks at a higher level than before. To do this, we need two things:

- work
- feedback.

Teams that want to learn, need to be doing the work that is relevant for now and next. That is how they will be able to develop their evolving and emerging skills. My preferred definition of feedback is *information that helps improve performance*. As teams get and share this information, they can adjust and develop the work that they do to improve their performance – and so the cycle goes.

If your teams are not keeping up with emerging and evolving skills, ask these two simple questions:

- Are we doing the right work?
- Are we getting the right feedback?

### *Unlearning*

This may be the most challenging aspect of learning in teams. It speaks directly to the idea of expiring skills – those skills that have served us well in the past, but are no longer relevant.

The challenge here is that we need to be able to acknowledge that what got us to where we are will not get us to where we want to be. We need to be able to leave behind many of the things that we have moved towards mastery of. Unfortunately, it is very easy to master obsolete skills. In hindsight, it seems clear, but at the time it may not.

Compared to their peak, there are very limited demands for skills such as blacksmiths, steam train drivers and telephone switchboard operators. Changes in technology and social behaviour have made those skills largely redundant. What is less obvious is which skills are expiring in our teams right now.

Without going into detail or attempting to gaze into a crystal ball, I can say with confidence that there will be shifts in what is demanded of almost every team in every workplace over the coming years and through the course of the 2020s. Unlearning is the key to unlocking these skills. Firstly, by letting go of what we no longer need, we don't waste our energy, attention and time on mastering yesterday's skills. Secondly, we also free up cognitive and calendar space to develop evolving and emerging skills.

# CAPACITY

A good way to consider capability is as *skill level combined with capacity*. So often, we assume that because we or our team have the skills to meet a challenge we are facing, we will be able to achieve our goal. It is worth considering whether we also have sufficient capacity. It's often the case that teams are running low on capacity as opposed to lacking the skills.

Teams need to invest in creating the space, the habits and processes that allow them to have more capacity. In your team, it is likely to mean some decisions about how you work together, what work you will prioritise and how you can carve out time for regenerating energy (individually and collectively).

A dangerous assumption is that working better requires us to work harder and longer. Most of our teams are working as hard as we can and that makes the idea of better work either unobtainable or unappealing (if it means more hours of harder work). Decoupling working harder and working better in our mind could free us to move towards an optimal experience in our teams.

## WORKING HARDER AND LONGER ISN'T WORKING

A 2018 *Harvard Business Review* article by Michael Porter and Nitin Nohria[3] reported on the results of a study over 12 years looking at how CEOs spent over 60,000 hours (both work and non-work time). There were some fascinating results, including that:

- these CEOs worked on 79% of weekend days and on 70% of vacation days
- CEOs routinely described managing time as one of their greatest challenges
- in any given week, they spent 72% of their total work time in meetings.

While we may not all be CEOs, many of us will empathise with these trends. Work is increasingly done outside of 'business hours'. Making the best use of our time is a constant challenge.

What all of this means is that statistically, there is a good chance that despite working long, working hard and being busy... you and your teams are often left with a sense of not making the progress that you would like to. Progress is a great motivator in teams. Hence, it makes sense that a lack of progress can diminish motivation.

**Creating opportunities for uninterrupted time to focus on complex problems and find solutions that matter is as essential as it is difficult to achieve. It will, however, set your teams on the path to sustainable high performance.**

Teams need to pay closer attention to the capacity at both individual and collective levels in order to achieve consistently high levels of performance that are able to be maintained for the long run and are not going to lead to burnout along with the associated health and business impacts.

## OVERCOMMITMENT IS MARRIED TO UNDERESTIMATION

Is your team overcommitted? A *lot* of teams are. It happens easily and often. In a busy, complex and fast-paced world we are being asked to achieve more – with fewer resources, less time and less clarity. In short, this increasing speed of operation combined with decreasing predictability (both inside and outside of our organisations) is increasing the complexity of the environments that we are working in.

Overcommitment is married to underestimation. They don't always hang out together, but overcommitment and underestimation are committed life partners. Overcommitment is usually the product of underestimating one or more of these things:

- the time, complexity or size of the task to be done
- our capacity to complete the task
- what we are already committed to.

Complex answers rarely have simple solutions. Here are three ideas that can help overcommitted teams.

### *Get better at noticing*

One of my all-time favourite phrases working with teams is... 'What are you noticing?'. It's so useful in so many ways. Awareness allows us to make choices and take action.

As teams get better at noticing, they can become better at making choices and taking actions that avoid overcommitment. Your team can have overt conversations and talk about:

- the signs of overcommitment (How does it feel? How do we respond?)
- the causes of overcommitment (How did we get here? Try not to judge – this is about learning.)
- the actual time, resources and capacity of tasks (What does

it really take to get this done? Is what we are trying to do achievable and sustainable?)

Pay more attention to these things and you can move towards better estimating what the team can confidently and realistically commit to.

### Do what is essential

A few years back, my word for the year was 'essential'. It came after I read the book *Essentialism* by Greg McKeown.[4] That year, when I was faced with choices of what to do, I would often ask myself, 'Is this essential?'. By essential, I meant does this help me make progress on something of significance to me. It helped me reduce commitments in my life as I realised that I had spread myself way too thin and been mediocre at many things. I still need to remind myself of this often – weekly if not daily.

The same thing happens in our teams. We are overwhelmed by requests (probably more like demands) from many different stakeholders. Teams can easily find themselves overcommitted as a result. We discussed the value of a purpose that is owned, compelling and questionable in Chapter 4. The absence of this hurts our teams. When our team is faced with decisions on what to do, it is very difficult for us to say no to something if we aren't clear on what our purpose is. We end up saying yes and getting overcommitted.

Getting clear on your team's purpose helps teams to make decisions and take the actions that are essential.

### Have better systems, not bigger goals

I find myself consistently quoting James Clear and his book, *Atomic Habits*.[5] One favourite quote that I share with the teams I work with often is this: 'You don't rise to the level of your goals, you fall to the level of your systems'.

I interpret this as another estimation error. We overestimate the impact of our willpower and good intentions. At the same time, we underestimate what we are currently committed to and the influence of environmental factors.

When I was part of an in-house learning team, my mate Max used to talk about us having a 'bookshelf' in reference to our capacity. Each project that we were asked to take on was a book in his analogy. Max would say that if someone wants us to put a book on the shelf and it's already full, then we'll need to take one off. He was right. Our ability to realistically assess our capacity as a team allowed us to have better conversations with stakeholders who wanted everything yesterday and helped us deliver good work on or before time, on or under budget.

If you can design a better way that your team commits to work and pay attention to capacity, you will be able to reduce the anxiety and underperformance caused by overcommitment and underestimation.

## RESILIENCE IS A TEAM GAME

Resilience is one of those overused words in modern business circles. It has become thrown around with little care and, at worst, on occasions it is used to imply that individuals are somehow internally deficient if they can't handle what is expected of them. That is, organisations provide some sort of resilience training or communications strategy and then suggest when their employees are experiencing the health and performance setbacks that 'people need to be resilient'.

There is some truth to that. As individuals, we can help ourselves to be increasingly able to cope with the demands of our work and life. It's not enough, though.

One of the 'laws' of behavioural economics is that behaviour is a function of the person and their environment. In the context of resilience, we tend to place too much emphasis on the person and not enough on the environment. This is a mistake. As Adam Grant says in his book, *Give and Take*, 'three decades of research show that receiving support from colleagues is a robust antidote to burnout.'[6] In other words, resilience is a team game.

To understand this a bit further, we need to look into what resilience is and how teams can create an environment for this. While there are many definitions that refer to resilience, the general theme is that resilience is a quality that allows someone (or something) to return to its intended purpose, structure and operation after experiencing change or a disruption. A more nuanced and systemic definition comes via The Resilience Alliance... 'Resilience is the capacity of a system to absorb disturbance and reorganise while undergoing change so as to still retain essentially the same function, structure, identity, and feedbacks.'[7]

## In other words, resilience requires capacity.

One of the great benefits of operating as a team (as opposed to a group) is the ability to adapt and be responsive to changes. Teams are resilient, groups are robust – they work in specific conditions, but don't respond well outside of those situations.

Having spare capacity is an important element of achieving resilience in teams. We can't adapt to additional or new challenges if all of our energy, attention and time is being consumed by existing demands. Metaphorically, it's like the straw that breaks the camel's back. So often we think that as individuals or teams we are broken by the final change. In actual fact, it's more likely that we are overburdened and that better managing our capacity

– knowing what we can handle and having some buffer up our sleeve to temporarily absorb disturbance – is not weak, it builds in structural strength.

## MANAGING MOJO, BABY!

In 1999, Austin Powers and Dr Evil introduced me to the concept of mojo. It existed before then, but the Austin Powers sequel was my introduction to it. At first, I assumed that it was just a funny word used as part of an intentionally nonsensical film plot. It is both those things – as well as something far more.

I have come to the conclusion that this is something that many of us can spend more time prioritising for ourselves and others. Here is why that is – and how you can prioritise it in your teams.

### What is mojo?

Turns out that the word has been around for longer than 20 years, but when I watched that again recently as research for this book (yep, I searched YouTube for Austin Powers clips as 'research'), I was taken aback. It has a lot more depth than I had given it credit for. The way that mojo is defined is very close to how I use the term 'character': the aspects of who we are that make us unique and distinct from everyone else.

### Why does mojo matter?

The things that make us unique are important. They reaffirm our self-worth and allow us to express it in a way that adds value for others. In 1970, Abraham Maslow (of the famous hierarchy of needs) wrote this:

*Musicians must make music, artists must paint, poets must write if they are to ultimately be at peace with themselves.*

*What humans can be, they must be. They must be true to their own nature.*[8]

This is what accessing our mojo does. It helps us be true to our nature as individuals. In a team setting, it helps us foster psychological safety and feel like we belong. It makes it easier for us to bring our best.

### Prioritising mojo

For that reason, mojo is a great thing for teams to be focused on. It feels self-indulgent, but is far from it. All of us need to connect into our unique talents. Ignoring it is an act of self-sabotage that many of us are guilty of. Do that for yourself and with your team and the results are likely to surprise you.

By prioritising mojo, we increase and free up capacity at both individual and collective levels.

## STRENGTHS

The final thing that we need to consider in our team's capability is the use of strengths in teams. Much like the idea of resilience, the concept of strengths is often used too much or without a full appreciation of what that means. There is value in getting clear about what strengths are (and aren't) as well as what the best way to work with strengths in teams is.

A 2011 paper by Alex Wood and others[9] defines strengths as 'characteristics that allow a person to perform well or at their best'. This definition reinforces this important point:

# Strengths are not simply what you are good at.

While there are many definitions floating around, it's clear that none of the useful ones stop at just the ability to do something well. Most of us have experienced something in our life that we are good at, but don't particularly enjoy. For me, when I was dating Rebecca (now my wife), I impressed her with my ability to clean the stovetop. This has become part of my responsibilities and I'm still good at it – but it doesn't light me up! It's not an activity that I would often choose to do or one that energises me. In a work setting, it's easy to become very good at things that do not reflect the best version of you.

Research into strengths is still emerging and so it is difficult to find a unifying or common definition. I have presented my position here and encourage you to consider where you stand on this. One thing that will influence your ability to apply the use of strengths in teams is how you define it.

Thinking about the definition above, it is the element of allowing someone to 'perform at their best' that is interesting. Depending on how you frame it, this could be about the observable performance. Given that a strengths-based approach is associated with the idea of promoting flourishing – *optimal performance* – it is useful to consider strengths in the following ways:

### State more than a trait

If you believe that strengths are a trait (inherent within a person), you will look to identify and exploit individual and collective strengths. If you believe that strengths are more state-related (transient and able to be cultivated), you will spend more time developing the strengths of your team. At this point in the book, you will probably not be surprised that I am in the camp of strengths being a state more than a trait.

### Give energy, don't drain

Most people have activities that energise them and others that seem to drain their energy. Strengths are often the things that reaffirm the values that we hold or the image that we have of ourselves, which makes us more likely to put in our best effort for longer. This can happen even if we are not particularly good at the skill. Paying attention to what energises team members and not just what they are good at is useful.

### Enable performance

Strengths enable performance in a few ways. A strength not only encourages our best effort, it also makes us keen to learn, adapt and apply certain activities. In those ways, strengths enable individuals to not only perform at current levels, but to also sustain their performance.

### Acknowledge weaknesses

One criticism of a strengths-based approach to leading teams is that it ignores weaknesses. This is not automatically the case. For a strengths-based approach to be most effective, it requires the acknowledgement of weaknesses. It is an important factor to consider. As we will soon discuss, the over-utilisation of a strength can actually manifest as a vulnerability.

## COMPLEMENTARY STRENGTHS, NOT JUST INDIVIDUAL STRENGTHS

To date, most emphasis on the use of strengths has focused on using individual team members' strengths. There is value in this approach and it is likely to benefit the way that many teams work. Where the magic happens is when we can combine those strengths to form something greater than the sum of their parts.

A 2019 article by Aaron McEwan in *Inside HR*[10] suggests that our teams can learn from superhero movies (who are increasingly turning up in movies as a band rather than solo artists) – by using complementary skills and strengths to deal with the size and complexity of the challenges faced.

Apart from Batman, I'm not that into superhero movies but I get the point. McEwan references the same research about complementary leadership conducted by Gartner that I mentioned earlier in this book. Leaders have the most positive impact when they are able to partner effectively. Once again, we can see that the environment that we are operating in is best suited to:

- a small group of people
- with complementary skills
- who are committed to a common purpose, performance goals and approach
- for which they hold themselves mutually accountable.

This might look familiar – it is *literally* the definition of teams presented in this book and by Katzenbach and Smith. It's teams who win – and leveraging complementary strengths is a great way to shift the dial on team performance.

## THE STRENGTH OF THE TEAM

One of my favourite quotes on teams of all time is from Phil Jackson. He is a basketball coach from the USA and has won 11 championships with two separate teams. He has come to prominence again in 2020 through the Netflix series on the 1997/98 Chicago Bulls season called *The Last Dance*. Here is what Phil Jackson has been quoted as saying...

# 'The strength of the team is each member. The strength of each member is the team.'

I love this. I love, love, love this.

It has such depth and value. In some ways, it reflects the spirit of Ubuntu that I mentioned in Chapter 4. It speaks directly to the fact that our teams need the best of each of us and that the best of each of us is a reflection of the people that we are surrounded by. Our job in teams is to bring our best and encourage others to bring theirs. Keeping this pithy phrase in mind helps teams and team members focus on what it takes to reach great heights.

## OVERPLAYED STRENGTHS AS A WEAKNESS

There is a big risk and opportunity cost for teams that ignore the individual and collective strengths of team members. It would be remiss of me to ignore the fact that there are risks on the other side of the coin as well. It is possible that strengths can be overplayed at both individual and team levels.

A 2009 article by two Roberts (Kaplan and Kaiser) in the *Harvard Business Review*[11] explores this idea by referencing their '25 years of leadership consulting and our analysis of 360-degree feedback on about 1,200 middle and senior managers (completed by nearly 15,000 co-workers over the course of a decade)'. Here are some of the key points that are useful for the performance of all teams.

- Overused strengths have negative impacts on two aspects of team performance: vitality (defined as morale, engagement, and cohesion) and productivity (quantity and quality of output). In the language of this book it is both cohesion and capability.

- Once you overplay a strength, you're at risk of diminished capacity on the opposite pole. In other words, using your preferences too much can expose you to underutilising other useful aspects of your performance.
- They found that 55% of the managers were rated by co-workers as using too much of at least one leadership attribute, but the majority of those managers did not rate themselves as overdoing that attribute.

This final point may be the most pertinent. We are often not great at recognising when our own strengths have been overplayed. For example, a leader who is visionary and sees the big picture may take too long to implement actions. Inversely, a team member with a gift for getting work done may not spend enough time considering the larger implications of their actions. What makes it more complicated is that those strengths are often the reasons that we are a part of the team and are often things that we cherish.

Once again, this is where the idea of operating as a team shows its value. Finding a way to share and deploy collective and complementary strengths allows teams to choose when to deploy their various strengths – when we need our visionary colleagues and other times when we just need to get $#!+ done! Designing and operating through the lens of complementary strengths reinforces that *all of us are better than any one of us.*

## RECAP

# CAPABILITY IS COMPLEX

A team's capability needs to be seen through the lenses of the team's context and is only ever realised through the ability of that team to develop cohesion. The skills that are required for teams are never static. In response to shifts in context, skills are constantly evolving, emerging or expiring and teams need to operate with this in mind.

Just as importantly, skills are only a part of what a team's capability incorporates. Too often, teams do not pay enough attention to their capacity. Without capacity, teams cannot perform at an optimal level at any given time and are unable to be resilient to disruptions.

Finally, deploying strengths is an important part of team performance. This needs to be done with more nuance than simply pandering to each individual's preference. To be greater than the sum of their parts, teams need to develop ways of working that allow for complementary strengths to be acknowledged, valued and expressed.

We need to look at a team's capability in a more holistic way. What teams can achieve together is more than the sum of the skills that individual team members possess at any given time. To leverage the benefits of working as a team, it's important to recognise the surprising complexity of a team's capability.

# REVIEW QUESTIONS

Use these questions to capture your own thoughts or facilitate a conversation with your team.

## SKILLS

- What are some skills that are *evolving* for your team – and how can you support their development?
- What are some skills that are *emerging* for your team – and how can you support their acquisition?
- What are some skills that are *expiring* for your team – and how can you support their retirement?

## CAPACITY

- What have you and your team been overcommitted to?
- Are you and your team clear on what is essential?
- What is one thing that would help your team have a better system for committing to tasks as they arrive?

## STRENGTHS

- Does each member know and articulate *their own strengths* in the team?
- Does each member know and articulate *the strengths of others* in the team?
- How well do your teams leverage each other's strengths in response to the context of what is required?

## ACTIVITY – USER MANUAL

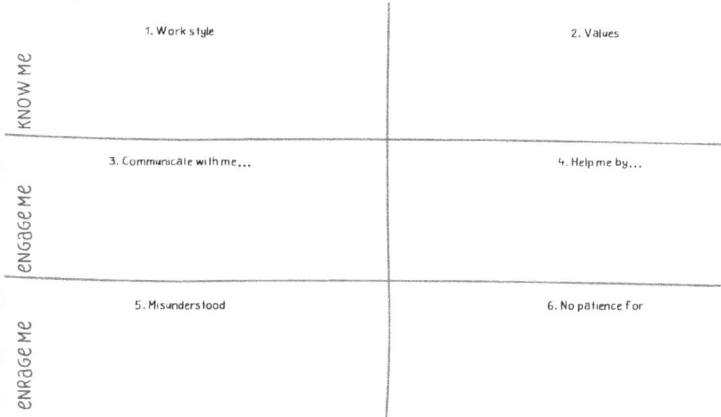

|  | 1. Work style | 2. Values |
|---|---|---|
| **KNOW ME** | | |
| **ENGAGE ME** | 3. Communicate with me... | 4. Help me by... |
| **ENRAGE ME** | 5. Misunderstood | 6. No patience for |

### PURPOSE

Use this activity as a way of:

- helping participants articulate important information about themselves
- encouraging self-reflection and self-awareness in team members
- facilitating a conversation about how team members can best leverage collective capability.

### WHAT YOU'LL NEED

- one sheet of paper per participant (any size A4 to flip chart)
- pens/markers for participants

## INSTRUCTIONS

### STEP 1
Ask participants to create a six-box grid on their page (as per example provided)

### STEP 2
Ask participants to place the answers to these questions in the corresponding numbered box.
1. How do you describe your work style?
2. What do you value?
3. What is the best way to communicate with you?
4. How can others help you?
5. What do you not have patience for?
6. What do people misunderstand about you?

### STEP 3
Ask participants to reflect on what this means for them and:
- how they are currently turning up in their teams
- how they would like to turn up in their teams.

### STEP 4 (OPTIONAL)
Facilitate a conversation with other team members and explore how you can assist each other to be a better team member.
- Recommend that these conversations are 1:1.
- For larger groups or teams it is recommended to engage a skilled facilitator.

# PART III

# WHAT WILL BE

Part III is dedicated to what will be for teams in three distinct ways.

First we'll explore what happens for teams when they are able to combine each of the elements of the Team Performance System. We will see that when teams are able to operate with high levels of capability, cohesion and context, team members can take actions that are:

- the right tasks
- performed better together
- prioritising the needs of the team over individual needs.

Then we'll take a look over the horizon at what some influences that are likely to shape the next decade or two of team performance. These include the rise of the gig economy, the increasing diversity of teams and the broadening applications of artificial intelligence. The good news about these trends is that even if they don't come fully to fruition, moving towards them will give you an advantage in current circumstances – and will position your teams ahead of many others if and when they do come to prominence.

Finally, we look at what will be required at all levels within organisations to make the most of teams. Briefly, each of these questions will be answered:

- What do team members need to do in order to add and receive value from the multiple teams that they are a part of?
- How do leaders need to turn up to bring people together and elevate performance?
- Can organisations leverage the benefits of teaming at scale?

# CHAPTER 7

# IMPLEMENTATION

In this chapter, we are going to look at:
- combining the elements of the Team Performance System
- the benefits of a humble swagger and teamership
- what fractals have to do with it all.

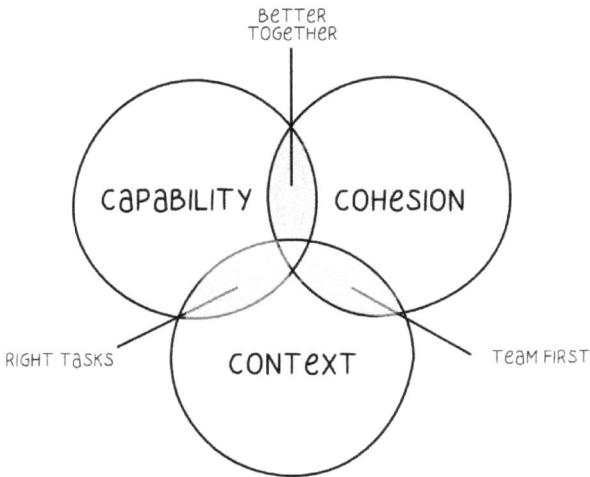

*Putting the Team Performance System into action.*

I n an episode of the US version of *The Office*, Michael Scott, the insecure and incompetent boss of Dunder Mifflin, is driving a rental car with his colleague, Dwight. They are in unfamiliar territory and as a result their navigation is done purely through the GPS system. At one point, the instruction from the GPS is to turn right and the two of them get into an argument. Dwight thinks it's a bad idea. Michael is determined to follow the instructions. He yells, 'The GPS lady knows what she is doing!!!'.

Then he drives into a lake.

It's a pretty funny incident and one that we would like to believe only happens in the fictionalised world of TV comedy. Unfortunately, that's not the case. There are regular news stories from around the world of how people unquestioningly follow the instructions of their GPS into lakes, rivers or buildings.

While there is an argument to be made that the GPS systems could be more accurate, they cannot be expected to be 100% accurate and up to the second (although they are even better now with traffic level indicators and so on). It is not unreasonable to ask drivers to respond to what is in front of them. A GPS provides highly reliable direction based on the information available at the time. The safety of the vehicle still relies on the driver taking responsibility, being aware and responsive to what is around them.

## DECISIONS AND ACTIONS

So it is with the Team Performance System. It will provide you with useful guidance and assist your teams to continue to improve. It is designed to be responsive and adaptable, but the performance of the team still depends on the team making the right decisions and taking the right actions based on what is in front of them.

A team's capability and cohesion only ever exist in context. When we support visibility and understanding of context, we support the development of the right capabilities and the right cohesion that drives performance in that context. When we get all three factors, our teams and team members can perform:

- the right tasks
- better together
- prioritising the needs of the team over individual needs.

Ultimately, teams that achieve important objectives consistently make decisions and take actions that serve the team.

## RIGHT TASKS

When teams have clarity on their context and possess the capability to deliver on what is required of them, they are able to choose and implement the right tasks. Members are able to readily identify opportunities to progress the team towards its objectives, to minimise risks that may jeopardise achieving those objectives and take action on the things that are going to have the most impact.

A great example of what this looks like is the approach that the Ritz-Carlton takes with its employees (who they refer to as 'Ladies & Gentlemen'!). Many of us have heard of the Ritz-Carlton. Certainly, a lot more of us have heard of it than have stayed there! They are a network of hotels and resorts at the upper end of luxury. Here is what they do: each Lady & Gentleman at The Ritz-Carlton, at all levels, is empowered to spend up to $2,000 per guest, per incident.

That sounds extravagant – even for an extravagant place! $2,000? Per guest, per incident? That could get very expensive very quickly. Turns out it doesn't. The $2,000 rarely gets spent.

So why do it? It's about the signal that this sends. It is almost literally putting their money where their mouth is. It's more useful than saying that they trust their staff, it's tangibly demonstrating that.

In reading this through the lens of the Team Performance System, you can see that it is a combination of capability and context that allow this empowerment to arise. *Capability* looks like no need for sign off or go through administrative processes and access to the resources to execute the task. *Context* looks like clearly aligning this approach to the purpose of the teams – and delivering customer experiences.

The result is world class hospitality.

It's a hard thing to get into our heads after the prevailing messages we have grown up with were that performance is a result of providing extrinsic motivation (financial or status punishments and rewards) and keeping tight control over what is and is not acceptable in our teams. The Ritz-Carlton approach shows the benefit of

- getting people on your team that are a good fit for what you need to do
- providing them with the resources to do their job
- having them understand what the team stands for and then...
- trusting them enough to get out of their way!

The impact of this type of approach is significant for team members, leaders and organisations.

### Team members

Operating in this way increases the autonomy of team members. We know from much research into self-determination theory that autonomy has been closely related to intrinsic motivation (which is far more powerful and effective in the long run than extrinsic motivation such as money or status). This becomes an upward spiral. As team members make more decisions and take more actions autonomously, they notice they learn more about what works (and what doesn't), improve their decisions and actions and so on.

### Leaders

For leaders, while this might feel a little bit like 'taking your hands off the steering wheel', it is necessary. The number one complaint of many leaders is that they can't get the time and space they need to focus on strategic objectives because they are caught in the details of day-to-day operations. Providing team members with the ability to get the right tasks done more often without input frees leaders up. This approach doesn't mean that leaders are never involved in decision-making with their teams. It means that leaders can get out of the detail and remain involved when a decision needs to be made with the leader's input.

### Organisations

For organisations, apart from the employee engagement that comes with autonomy, one of the biggest benefits of team members being able to work on the right tasks is that the work becomes more responsive to customer needs. Decentralising decision-making for some (not all) aspects of operations means that teams and individuals are able to be more innovative and also more resilient to rapid changes and disruption as the decision-making process does not have to go 'up and down the chain of command'.

## BETTER TOGETHER

As we know, one of the main benefits of teams is that they are greater than the sum of their parts. They deliver outcomes collectively that members could not achieve independently – in less time, to a higher standard or on a larger scale.

## Teams can answer the question of 'what can we achieve together that we could not do separately?'

That doesn't always mean that teams are without conflict. In fact, teams that are doing great work need to have conflict. The conflict needs to be productive and constructive (not destructive). It needs to be about the ideas, not the people. The team needs to be robustly debating new ways of working or exploring new solutions to problems that are unprecedented.

To have a truly great team, you need both talent and the ability to harness that talent. A way you might think of this is as the ability to both *task* (get work done) and *team* (get work done together).

*Task* is the individual capability and team the ability to be cohesive. The lure of always trying to find the most talented individuals in your field is strong. It's always tempting to find someone who has a track record of success in other settings and add them to your team. It's a game that you may never win, as in most fields there will continue to be people improving their individual capability. *Team* is the ability to create an environment that supports individuals that can and do work well together is important.

### TEAM FIRST

To team up effectively requires individuals to consider the group and not just themselves. This actually requires a lot more than platitudes or nice words on a wall. It requires individuals to be vulnerable, expose themselves to some risk and to feel like there is value in being a part of the group. It is a form of sacrifice to contribute to the greater good. We will do it when the benefit outweighs that sacrifice.

As you read through what it takes to effectively put the team first, you will see elements of both cohesion and context. In terms of cohesion, the willingness to put the team first comes as a result of psychological safety and connections. This means that as individuals, team members see the value in being a part of the team.

## Cohesion means that members are willing. Context means that they are able.

Team members are able to make choices and take actions that prioritise the needs of the team over their own needs when they:

- see their individual identity reflected in the team's collective identity
- have a clear understanding of the purpose that the team serves.

It should be clear that this is not altruism. Relying on altruism is a risky and flawed strategy to adopt for team performance. Relying on people to do the right thing by the team simply because they are told it would be nice for others is not a long-term path to success to. What putting the team first requires is for individual members to believe and experience that it is in their interest for the team to succeed. Ironic, right? *To make it all about the team, make sure individuals are getting what they need!*

One of my clients is a civil contracting company that specialise in demolition of industrial and commercial buildings. That means that they have a lot of specialised (and very expensive) equipment to get their work done. Given that there is limited equipment, they need to coordinate which project uses each piece at which time. Most of the time, because they are good at their work, they are able to schedule it so that each site can use the equipment sequentially. Occasionally, there are times when one piece of equipment is needed by two sites (delays caused by weather or other contractors are common reasons).

Traditionally, this was the source of arguments or frustration between projects. It would require some counselling and mediation skills from management before some sort of arrangement was made (that led to at least one party being frustrated). This was a result of:

- each project seeing themselves as a team and not really feeling connected to other projects
- a precedent that the project leader had to advocate strongly on behalf of their project to get the equipment that they needed.

This still happens a bit. What is increasingly happening is that when these schedule conflicts arise, project leaders are now speaking to each other and negotiating directly. Increasingly, they are coming to acceptable and less frustrating solutions.

This has brought about a number of benefits:

- The project leaders are working together across sites more as a collective team and starting to identify themselves as a part of that team as well as their project team.
- This has increased awareness of other projects so that people know what is happening on those sites and can plan more proactively.
- Over time, all of the projects have benefited from other projects being flexible with resources and are hence more likely to make a similar sacrifice themselves.

In other words, the ability to support cohesion and context simultaneously has demonstrated benefits at both individual and (multiple) team levels. In most organisations, a version of this exists. There are often limited resources (money, equipment or even meeting rooms) and the ability of individuals to share those well is both a competitive advantage and a reflection of behaviour that is 'team first'.

## WHAT THIS MEANS FOR INDIVIDUALS, LEADERS AND ORGANISATIONS

I'm a huge fan of the 1980s movie trilogy *Back to the Future*. In case you are unfamiliar with them or haven't watched the movies in a while, all that you need to know is that it centres on the adventures of a teenager, Marty, who travels through time courtesy of a home-made time machine that his friend, Doc, has invented.

In the second movie, Marty and Doc travel forward to 2015. From the 1980s, they imagined what this distant time might hold in store. They had some hits and some misses.

They accurately predicted technology included things like drones, tablet computers and fingerprint identification. Unfortunately for them (and us), they were wrong about hoverboards, self-lacing shoes and flying cars.

The fact is that we don't know (and can't know) exactly what the future of work entails for all of us, but we can make some good predictions based on what we know is on the horizon. Here are three things that have been predicted and are worth taking your teams towards:

## EVEN MORE NEED FOR COLLABORATION

At a conference in 2018, during a Q&A session I asked the co-founder of Atlassian (my company crush that build software to support team performance), Scott Farquhar, the question, 'Why teams?'. He made a great point about offering solutions for what is *not* going to change over the next decade (a concept he had heard Jeff Bezos of Amazon talking about) and concluded his answer to my question by stating that...'It's always going to be hard to communicate and collaborate with people, so we focus on that problem. Until we get brain-to-brain communication, telepathy, I think that we're pretty safe that will be a problem'.

What is *not* likely to change over the next decade? The need for diverse teams to work together. There is every chance that our teams are going to become more diverse in every sense (not just demographics). Our teams are likely to become more cross-functional, more remote and even cross-organisational. All of that makes the ability to operate in teams a trend that is likely to be more valuable for the next decade or more.

### *The rise of artificial intelligence*

You don't need to know a lot about artificial intelligence (AI) and its implications to understand that rapid developments in this area means machines will be increasingly be able to learn, adapt, make decisions and take actions based on the masses of data that we are generating. You only need to consider the way that we use features like Siri or Google Maps to imagine what the next decade might bring in that space.

During the same Q&A session, Scott Farquhar spoke about the fact that the jobs most at risk of automation are those that can be done alone. Interestingly, he suggested that a highly skilled heart surgeon was more likely to be replaced than a team of emergency nurses at the same hospital. I don't know if that's true, but it makes sense to me. The reason being that tasks that are repeatable and predictable are more able to be learned and improved through the use of the data that is now available.

It's another instance of humans versus resources. The tasks that can be done by resources (machines and data centres) will be – efficiently, quickly and cheaply. For other tasks, elevating and leveraging the things that make humans unique – like language, communication and collaboration – is going to become increasingly valuable.

### The gig economy

We have seen the rise of companies like Uber and Deliveroo, which, despite their reach and revenue, don't actually have a very large number of employees on their books. They engage workers on an ad hoc basis, when and where work is needed. There is every indication that this trend is likely to continue to be driven by technological, social and economic factors. As soon as there are platforms connecting enough people with solutions matched to organisations with problems, 'gig working' becomes increasingly prevalent. In that instance, employers or bosses doing the hiring and allocation of work can no longer rely on hierarchy and employment contracts for access to the best talent. If you want to do great work, you need to be able to rapidly form high performing teams taking on interesting projects and offering the ability for people to work when and where they choose.

The good news about these three trends is that even if they don't come fully to fruition, moving towards them will give you an advantage right now – as well as position your teams ahead of many others if they do arise.

# CULTIVATING FOLLOWERSHIP – WHAT WILL BE REQUIRED OF LEADERS

The leadership that our teams need is no longer that which is reliant upon authority, positional power or crude applications of generic reward (and punishment) strategies. What we need for high performing teams in the 2020s is a style of leadership that *cultivates followership*. This might be different from the picture that you have in your mind of what leadership is, so here is a very brief explanation:

### Followership

If nobody is buying, you're not selling. If nobody is learning, you aren't teaching. If nobody is following, you're not leading. Irrespective of your title or job description, leadership inherently requires that others make decisions and take actions that align to a direction that you have laid out.

### Cultivating

Cultivating followership means acknowledging that we do the things on a consistent basis that make us more likely to be followed. Gardening is an apt metaphor. I'm not a gardener, but I can get my head around the fact that we can't guarantee the success of any flowers that we plant – ever. What we can do is plant them in suitable soil, in a place that gets the right amount of sun, at the right time of year and then water, feed and prune them appropriately. After all of that, we have given the flowers their best chance. We can't change drought, or flood, or fire or a bug that may prevent those flowers from reaching their potential.

So it is with leading teams in a modern world. Success can't be guaranteed because of the inherent complexity of the task at hand. Leaders can only consistently make the decisions and take the actions that make success and growth more likely in their teams.

It is important to point out that I am referring to leadership (the behaviours that cultivate followership) and not the appointed boss of a team. In the best teams, there is shared leadership. Using the definition above does not limit the behaviours of leadership to the appointed leader. The question becomes how each of us can cultivate followership.

## ENTER THE HUMBLE SWAGGER

Many leaders rise to their leadership roles through their technical ability or their ability to develop business. These abilities are also a strength for many leaders – they can speak from experience and with credibility. We want and hope that our leaders will possess and instil confidence. We want our leaders to swagger.

Too much swagger, however, and leaders are at danger of coming across with hubris, arrogance and in extreme cases, narcissism. There is a raft of evidence that demonstrates that such behaviours can be damaging to teams and organisations.

Excessive swagger has been prevalent across industries. This has spawned new thinking in recent times around the importance of humility in leadership. Research supports that leading with humility is correlated with many positive outcomes within teams, including creativity and information sharing. In an operating environment where complexities and rates of change continue to increase, it is less likely that leaders have all the answers. We need our leaders to:

- acknowledge that they cannot possibly have all the answers
- ask good questions
- foster curiosity
- be honest when the answer is 'I don't know'.

We want our leaders to be humble. Too much humility, however, and leaders run the risk of not being visible enough or their perspectives not being visible enough to cultivate followership.

So where does that leave us?

## Teams need leaders to have swagger. Teams need leaders to be humble.

Great! Except for the inherent contradiction, of course.

As a leader, it often feels like humble and swagger live at opposite end of the same spectrum. A bit like a see saw – if one end goes down, another must come up. The secret to leaders who master the humble swagger is that they realise that it is not a choice of humble *OR* swagger. It is a process of trying to present with humility *AND* swagger. This shift in mindset allows leaders to accept the positive aspects of their experience and perspective while still acknowledging their limitations and ability to learn. They take a position based on their experience, and are also open to the views of their team. They give advice based on their extensive experience over many years and at the same time support ideas from less experienced team members.

The humble swagger points to a broader set of skills possessed by the best leaders. They are able to see and operate with paradoxes. They acknowledge that, very often, a weakness is when we overplay a strength. This turns up with many of the challenges that leaders are faced with regularly:

- Do I focus on results or relationships?
- Is quantity or quality of work more important?
- Is it best to be directive or supportive?

In almost all of these paradoxical questions, the answer is 'yes'. As we have seen throughout this book, context is what guides these decisions in the best team environments.

As a leader, if we adopt a mindset that we can only be one or the other, we limit the range of scenarios that we are effective in. To be more effective in more situations, leaders need to be able to be both directive *AND* supportive, to focus on relationships *AND* results. At different times, they may need to pull one lever more than another. The most effective leaders are those who have the broadest range of skills. More specifically, the best leaders can choose and apply a broad range of skills in the right situation.

## TEAMERSHIP – WHAT WILL BE REQUIRED OF TEAM MEMBERS

How many teams are you on?

Research in 2011 suggested that up to 95% of workers across a range of industries in the United States and Europe were members of more than one team simultaneously and that it is common for an individual to be a member of 'five, ten, or twelve or more teams at a time' within some organisations.[1] Most conversations on teams refer to intact teams and do not make explicit reference to multiple team membership. This is a huge missed opportunity – and risk.

Our job descriptions, email signatures and LinkedIn profile might not yet acknowledge it, but we need to acknowledge that the reality that we are all on many teams. That means that there is a competitive advantage if individuals are able to identify the teams that they are part of, their best contribution in each of those teams and how to bring out the best in others across those teams.

This is the rise of teamership. Teamership is the phrase that I use to capture *the art and science of being a great team member.*

The ability to be a great team member will continue to set individuals and organisations apart. I did research on this as part of my Masters of Business Coaching. I asked an academic version of this question: 'What does a great team member do?'

In his book *The Ideal Team Player,* Patrick Lencioni identifies the ideal team player as 'being humble, hungry and having people smarts'.[2] But what does that mean that they do? In my research, I asked people from range of teams across domains (sport and business), locations (including Australia, New Zealand, Japan and the United Kingdom) and sizes about their experiences of a great team member – and what they actually did. These people identified a range of practices rather than a list of specific behaviours that will work in all teams, in all settings, at all times.

It may be that there is no definitive list of individual practices that improves team effectiveness in all scenarios. This point was summarised by a participant who shared her perspective on being a great team member in the quote below:

## 'I think it's around, "What value can I bring to this team? What does this team need from me? How do I meet that need?" '

We can all benefit if we and our colleagues are willing and able to regularly ask and answer these questions. How can I be a better team member? How can I help others to be a better team member?

If each of us is a better team member, it's a great outcome for:
- Us as individuals – it is intrinsically rewarding to know that we

are making a positive contribution to the teams that we are a part of. It also makes us someone that others will choose to work with (which is a huge advantage for our careers).

- The teams that we are part of – this seems pretty obvious.
- The organisations that we work in – the more individuals in an organisation who have the flexibility to play different roles across different teams, the better an organisation is able to respond to the change in its environment.

Ultimately, teamership is about bringing our best to the teams that we are a part of and enabling others to bring their best. Developing these skills will set us apart.

## A NETWORK OF TEAMS – WHAT WILL BE REQUIRED OF ORGANISATIONS

In 2018, Margaret Luciano of Arizona State University and her fellow researchers looked into what they referred to as Multiteam Systems. Their paper was entitled 'Multiteam Systems: A Structural Framework and Meso-Theory of System Functioning'.3 For team nerds like me, it's thrilling stuff to get lost in. One practical implication is the fact that organisations are increasingly structuring themselves as a complex network of interdependent teams. Given what has already been covered about the world being less predictable and more complex than ever, it makes sense to move away from traditional hierarchical structures to more complex networks.

It's an idea that is explored in the book, *Team of Teams* (referenced several times already), which describes how the Joint US Forces changed their way of working from being one driven by command and control to operating as a team of teams. (Given the title, that's not a spoiler!) The catalyst for this change was that the best resourced, most well trained military forces known to ever exist were simply not operating in a way that was suited the environment the context they found themselves in.

What happened (eventually) is that the US military forces radically changed their way of working and ended up achieving more of their objectives. From a pragmatic perspective the ability to change the way that they operated meant increased effectiveness. Warfare is an arena where nobody ever really wins (all parties lose – and some lose more than others). Often, though, lessons learned in military circles make their way directly or indirectly into civilian life and can benefit society – through medicine, technology or in this case organisational performance.

In response to the COVID-19 pandemic, McKinsey released a paper entitled 'To weather a crisis, build a network of teams'.[4] The parallels are somehow simultaneously surprising and unsurprising. The point was basically the same. McKinsey suggest that, 'This dynamic and collaborative team structure can tackle an organisation's most pressing problems quickly.'

## OPERATING AS A NETWORK OF TEAMS

I doubt that McKinsey believe that changing the organisation chart will be enough on its own. At a team level, it's not enough to be called a team, we need to operate as one. On a larger scale, to get the benefit of a complex interconnected network of teams is a challenging process. More than the theoretical structure, it requires a way of working that challenges 150 years of assumptions in our societies. Assumptions that for most of that 150 years have led to success.

McKinsey in their paper and McChrystal in *Team of Teams* suggest slightly different processes of building towards operating in such a way. The McKinsey model describes a path to a network of teams that starts with one central team, grows through a hub and spoke setup and eventually evolves into a network of teams. *Team of Teams* describes a process through an organisational lens. From a hierarchical setup described as command through a hierarchical structure of interdependent teams to a team of interdependent teams.

**The common theme with both approaches is that they require an appropriate model of team performance to be scaled up.**

In the military, they were scaling up some of the best teams in the world at what they do – such as Navy SEAL and Army Ranger teams. The approach presented by McKinsey that grows from a single team outwards. Hence it is possible to see that the approach to team performance that is established there will make or break the success of the whole network. Let me be explicit about this – I am referring to the way that the team performs, not how well that team performs at any given point in time. Failure is an inevitable part of teaming at the pace the 2020s demand. The model of teaming needs to be dynamic and responsive, able to share information rapidly, experiment, learn and empower members.

If you're wondering which approach you might choose, I'll provide you with a not very subtle reminder that I've spent this book advocating for the Team Performance System that explicitly responds to context and is designed to allow teams to be greater than the sum of their parts!

# A MATHEMATICAL REALITY WOVEN INTO THE FABRIC OF THE UNIVERSE

In the Disney movie, *Frozen* (which, courtesy of my daughter's age, I became very familiar with from 2014 to 2017!) introduced me to the idea of fractals. At one point in the central song of the movie, 'Let it Go', Elsa sings about 'frozen fractals'. I have to admit that I didn't really know what they were. To be honest, I didn't pay much attention to it (I tried to ignore *Frozen* as much as I could). In 2018, I saw Eddie Woo (maths teacher extraordinare) present at TEDx event in Sydney. Fractals showed up again. As he described it, fractals involved a recursive pattern – where each segment of a whole is made up of smaller versions of the same shape. He made a very well constructed and considered case that these fractals existed throughout nature – in broccoli, in trees, in river deltas and in the patterns of our veins. Somehow, this concept was everywhere, hiding in plain sight – and we can learn how to see it.

What if we could apply this fractal thinking to teams and organisations as well? Turns out that we can. At the 2020 Evidence-Based Coaching Conference, I heard Dr Michael Cavanagh present something along this line of logic. In essence, he suggested that coaching was the process of facilitating different perspectives to be shared, heard and acknowledged to function in a way that is useful for the situation. When it got really interesting was when he suggested that it is the same for individuals, teams and organisations:

- Individuals are working with different perspectives internally – perhaps conflicting values or a shift in personal priorities.
- Teams are working with the diverse perspectives of multiple individuals.

- Organisations are working with the interaction of perspectives representative of different teams.

  Fractals again! The same process at different levels.

While this is a very simplistic view of an incredibly complex phenomenon, there is something in it. The ability to take on board different perspectives and then respond appropriately to a situation is what high performing teams do. This can be scaled up to an organisational level (and beyond). It can also go the other way and apply for individuals. Working at team level offers an opportunity to make the team members and the organisations function better.

## REFLECTION AND INFLECTION

So, you're here. At the end of the book. Thanks for making it!

Towards the end of a session or program with a team, I often facilitate a discussion about designed to make the best use of our time together – so that it is not just a nice bit of time away from 'real work'. I ask them to consider how they can make it meaningful, productive and lead to better work in the future. The phrase that I have landed on is 'Reflection and inflection'.

It's my suggestion for you at this point of the book also.

### Reflection

An intentional look at the content and themes of this book. What can you remember? What has resonated with you? What meaning did you make of what you read?

### *Inflection*

This part of the process is forward looking. This is my great wish for you. That this book provides you with whatever you need (inspiration, evidence, a framework or a point of reference) to make the teams that you work with better and to lead bravely, with compassion, humour and strength. How will you use this book to bring people together and elevate their performance?

### *My gratitude*

Finally, let me say a direct and sincere thanks to you. I am so glad that you have taken the time and effort to read these words – and get all of the way to the end. Your attention is a valuable resource and I am honoured that you have chosen to devote it to this book and this subject matter. I believe deeply in the positive impact that teams can have on individuals, organisations and societies.

If that is true for you, then I hope that this book has provided you with both a call to action and a path to action. That you will make mistakes, learn, fail and succeed. That along the way, you will learn about getting the most out of yourself and how others can do the same. That you will do the work to support your teams to be greater than the sum of their parts.

In other words, I hope that you will Team Up.

# REFERENCES

.

## CHAPTER 1: TEAMS AND HUMANITY

1. Kozlowski, S.W. and Ilgen, D.R., 2006. Enhancing the effectiveness of work groups and teams. *Psychological science in the public interest, 7*(3), pp. 77-124.
2. Katzenbach, J.R. and Smith, D.K., 1993. The discipline of teams. *Harvard Business Review. March–April. Boston: Harvard Business Press*, pp. 111-120.

## CHAPTER 2: WHAT IS REQUIRED

1. Tuckman, B.W., 1965. Developmental sequence in small groups. *Psychological Bulletin, 63*(6), p. 384.
2. Lencioni, P., 2002. *The Five Dysfunctions Of A Team.* San Francisco: Jossey-Bass.
3. O'Leary, M.B., Mortensen, M. and Woolley, A.W., 2011. Multiple team membership: A theoretical model of its effects on productivity and learning for individuals and teams. *Academy of Management Review, 36*(3), pp. 461-478.
4. Hayes, M., Chumney, F., Wright, C. and Buckingham, M., 2019. Global Study of Engagement.

## CHAPTER 3: COMPLEXITY

1.   Snowden, D.J. and Boone, M.E., 2007. A leader's framework for decision making. *Harvard Business Review, 85*(11), p. 68.
2.   Mathieu, J.E., Gallagher, P.T., Domingo, M.A. and Klock, E.A., 2019. Embracing complexity: Reviewing the past decade of team effectiveness research. *Annual Review of Organizational Psychology and Organizational Behavior, 6*, pp. 17-46.
3.   The power of many: How companies use teams to drive superior corporate performance, Ernst & Young Global Limited, 2013.
4.   Leading the social enterprise: Reinvent with a human focus, 2019. Deloitte Global Human Capital Trends, 2019.

## CHAPTER 4: CONTEXT

1.   https://www.mercedesamgf1.com/en/news/2020/03/formula-1-project-pitlane/ [Accessed 6 July 2020].
2.   Godin, S., 2011. *The dip: the extraordinary benefits of knowing when to quit (and when to stick)*. Hachette UK.
3.   Hackman, J.R., 2012. From causes to conditions in group research. *Journal of organizational Behavior, 33*(3), pp. 428-444.
4.   Hunt-Davis, B. and Beveridge, H., 2012. *Will it Make the Boat Go Faster?* Troubador.
5.   https://www.ted.com/talks/dan_ariely_how_to_change_your_behavior_for_the_better [Accessed 6 July 2020].
6.   McChrystal, G.S., Collins, T., Silverman, D. and Fussell, C., 2015. *Team of teams: New rules of engagement for a complex world*. Penguin.

## CHAPTER 5: COHESION

1. Pentland, A. (2012), 'The new science of building great teams', *Harvard Business Review* 90 (4), pp. 60–69.

2. Brown, A.J. and Harkins, S.G., 2020. Social Facilitation and Social Loafing: Opposite Sides of the Same Coin. In Individual Motivation within Groups (pp. 297-330). Academic Press.

3. https://www.gartner.com/en/human-resources/trends/reshaping-leadership-to-prepare-for-the-future [Accessed 3 June 2020].

4. Duhigg, C., 2016. What Google learned from its quest to build the perfect team. *The New York Times Magazine, 26,* p. 2016.

5. Edmondson, A. and Lei, Z., 2014. Psychological safety: The history, renaissance, and future of an interpersonal construct. *Annual Review of Organizational Psychology and Organizational Behavior, 1*(1), pp. 23-43.

6. Edmondson, A., 1999. Psychological safety and learning behavior in work teams. *Administrative science quarterly, 44*(2), pp. 350-383.

7. Schein E. 1993. How can organizations learn faster? The challenge of entering the green room. *Sloan Management Review* 34, pp. 85–92.

8. https://www.dnb.com/perspectives/small-business/failure-wall-encouraging-culture-success.html [Accessed 13 July 2020].

## CHAPTER 6: CAPABILITY

1. https://www.gartner.com/smarterwithgartner/get-a-grip-on-critical-skills/ [Accessed 14 July 2020].

2. https://www.forbes.com/sites/rogerdooley/2017/08/24/is-marketing-dead-or-starting-a-new-golden-age/#7ce87d004ce6 [Accessed 14 July 2020].

3. Porter, M.E. and Nohria, N., 2018. How CEOs manage time. *Harvard Business Review, 96*(4), pp. 42-51.

4. Mckeown, G 2014, *Essentialism : the disciplined pursuit of less,* Currency, An Imprint Of Crown Publishing Group, New York.

5. Clear, J 2018, *Atomic habits : tiny changes, remarkable results: an easy & proven way to build good habits & break bad ones,* Avery, an imprint of Penguin Random House, New York.

6. Grant, A.M. and Ebsco Publishing (Firm (2014). *Give and take: why helping others drives our success.* New York: Penguin Books.

7. Walker, B., C. S. Holling, S. R. Carpenter, and A. Kinzig. 2004. Resilience, adaptability and transformability in social–ecological systems. *Ecology and Society 9(2): 5.* [online] URL: http://www.ecologyandsociety.org/vol9/iss2/art5/ [Accessed 14 July 2020].

8. Maslow, A. H. (1970). Motivation and personality. New York: Harper & Row.

9. Wood, A.M., Linley, P.A., Maltby, J., Kashdan, T.B. and Hurling, R., 2011. Using personal and psychological strengths leads to increases in well-being over time: A longitudinal study and the development of the strengths use questionnaire. *Personality and Individual Differences, 50*(1), pp. 15-19.

10. https://www.insidehr.com.au/future-leadership/ [Accessed 14 July 2020].

11. Kaplan, R.E. and Kaiser, R.B., 2009. Stop overdoing your strengths. *Harvard Business Review, 87*(2), pp. 100-103.

## CHAPTER 7: IMPLEMENTATION

1. O'Leary, M.B., Mortensen, M. and Woolley, A.W., 2011. Multiple team membership: A theoretical model of its effects on productivity and learning for individuals and teams. *Academy of Management Review, 36*(3), pp. 461-478.

2. Lencioni, P.M., 2016. *The ideal team player: How to recognize and cultivate the three essential virtues.* John Wiley & Sons.

3. Luciano, M.M., DeChurch, L.A. and Mathieu, J.E., 2018. Multiteam systems: A structural framework and meso-theory of system functioning. *Journal of Management, 44*(3), pp. 1065-1096.

4. www.mckinsey.com. (n.d.). *To weather a crisis, build a network of teams.* https://www.mckinsey.com/business-functions/organization/our-insights/to-weather-a-crisis-build-a-network-of-teams [Accessed 25 Jul. 2020].

# KEEGANLUITERS.

Thank you for reading *Team Up*. I trust that it has provided you with plenty of food for thought about why and how to take a deliberate approach to team performance.

What you do from now will make the difference for the leaders and teams that you support. As we all have experienced, there is a big difference between *knowing* and *doing*.

I work with leaders, teams and organisations to help them walk the path applying the principles outlined in *Team Up*. If you would like to explore how one of my speaking, coaching or training offerings can help serve you in your context, get in touch via my website and let's chat!

## www.keeganluiters.com

As you can probably gather, I always welcome the opportunity to chat all things teams and performance – and the development of leaders to support that. To do that, connect with me on LinkedIn or email me on: keegan@keeganluiters.com

I look forward to continuing the conversation,

Keegan